Beyond Gender

Published by

The Woodrow Wilson Center Press

Washington, D.C.

Distributed by

The Johns Hopkins University Press

Baltimore and London

BETTY FRIEDAN

Beyond Gender

THE NEW POLITICS
OF WORK AND FAMILY

edited by Brigid O'Farrell

Woodrow Wilson Center Special Studies

The Woodrow Wilson Center Press
Editorial Offices
370 L'Enfant Promenade, S.W., Suite 704
Washington, D.C. 20024-2518
Telephone 202-287-3000, ext. 218

Distributed by
The Johns Hopkins University Press
Hampden Station
Baltimore, Maryland 21211
Telephone 1-800-537-5487

2 4 6 8 9 7 5 3 1

Library of Congress Cataloging-in-Publication Data

Friedan, Betty.
    Beyond gender : the new politics of work and family / Betty
Friedan : edited by Brigid O'Farrell.
        p.   cm.
    ISBN 0-943875-84-6 (cloth : alk. paper).
    1. Women employees—United States—Social conditions. 2. Married
women—Employment—United States. 3. Downsizing of organizations—
United States. 4. Displaced workers—United States. 5. Manpower
policy—United States. 6. United States—Economic policy.
I. O'Farrell, Brigid. II. Title.
HD6058.F72   1997
305.42' 0973—dc21   *97-25592*
                                                                  CIP

Design: Adrianne Onderdonk Dudden

The Woodrow Wilson International Center for Scholars

The Center is the living memorial of the United States of America to the nation's twenty-eighth president, Woodrow Wilson. Congress established the Woodrow Wilson Center in 1968 as an international institute for advanced study, "symbolizing and strengthening the fruitful relationship between the world of learning and the world of public affairs." The Center opened in 1970 under its own board of trustees.

In all its activities, the Woodrow Wilson Center is a nonprofit, nonpartisan organization, supported financially by annual appropriations from the Congress, and by the contributions of foundations, corporations, and individuals.

WOODROW WILSON CENTER SPECIAL STUDIES
The work of the Center's Fellows, Guest Scholars, and staff—and presentations and discussions at the Center's conferences, seminars, and colloquia—often deserve timely circulation as contributions to public understanding of issues of national and international importance. The Woodrow Wilson Center Special Studies series is intended to make such materials available by the Woodrow Wilson Center Press to interested scholars, practitioners, and other readers. In all its activities, the Woodrow Wilson Center is a nonprofit, nonpartisan organization, supported financially by annual appropriations from the U.S. Congress and by the contributions of foundations, corporations, and individuals. Conclusions or opinions expressed in Center publications and programs are those of the authors and speakers and do not necessarily reflect the views of the Center staff, Fellows, trustees, advisory groups, or any individuals or organizations that provide financial support to the Center.

Contents

Acknowledgments

I began my search in earnest for a new paradigm of women, men, and community in the summer of 1994 when I moved to Washington, D.C. I am indebted to Charles Blitzer, director, and the Fellows, Guest Scholars, and staff of the Woodrow Wilson International Center for Scholars for providing a stimulating and collegial atmosphere in which to develop my ideas and host my New Paradigm Seminar series. Moira Egan and Christina Carhart were especially helpful, and it has been a pleasure to work with Joseph Brinley, Jr., director of the Woodrow Wilson Center Press, and Carol Belkin Walker, senior editor.

I am grateful for the intellectual contributions and good friendship of Heidi Hartmann, economist, director of the Institute for Women's Policy Research, and MacArthur Fellow, who agreed to cochair the seminar with me and expand my thinking in economics. Encouragement and support were also provided by my dear friend Marty Lipset, Hazel Professor of Public Policy and Sociology at George Mason University and Senior Fellow at the Woodrow Wilson Center, who was a regular presenter and participant in the seminars and also introduced me to colleagues and students at George

Mason University who helped shape my ideas in and outside the classroom.

The narrative form for this volume began to emerge in conversations with Tina Brown about an article for the *New Yorker* on the 1996 Stand for Children demonstration being organized by my friend Marian Wright Edelman, founder and president of the Children's Defense Fund. During the second year of the seminar, I was urged on by Lucyann Geiselman, president of Mount Vernon College, who graciously made me a distinguished visiting professor at the college and so made it possible for me to try my ideas out with thoughtful, lively students. Brigid O'Farrell joined me there as a visiting fellow to edit the seminar transcripts and to help shape and edit the book. Cecilia Simons and Vanessa White worked hard and were, each in her own way, sources of calm and good humor, which I greatly appreciated as an article grew into a book. This entire endeavor would not have been possible without the generous financial support of Helen Hunt, and I thank her.

Finally I want to express my sincere thanks to all of the presenters and participants in the seminar sessions at the Woodrow Wilson Center. Many of them are quoted here, their contributions publicly acknowledged. I could not, however, include everyone. But it was indeed the many conversations that took place in the Woodrow Wilson Center library, the exchange of ideas back and forth about important topics and among such a diverse and distinguished group of policy makers, academics, researchers, and activists that made the seminars come alive. It is this sense of excitement and exchange that I have tried to convey here as we move beyond gender to the new politics of work and family.

Betty Friedan

Beyond Gender

1

DEFINING A PARADIGM SHIFT

I am having fruit and cottage cheese for lunch with a new friend at some innocuous spa-lunch place on Madison Avenue, near her bank. She happens to be the top woman at her bank, no other woman anywhere near her level, and she gets lonesome at lunchtime. The guys at her level at her bank all go out together, the men at any level don't have lunch with the women anymore. Some new kind of sex discrimination? "Oh no," she says, "it's just that there's so much talk about sexual harassment suits these days. No one knows what is or isn't, so they figure, why risk it."

But my friend isn't looking for feminist advice. What is really beginning to get her down is that her husband, who was downsized at one of our biggest corporations three years ago, hasn't been able to find a job and has almost stopped looking. "I'm carrying it all," she says. "It's okay, we'll make it. But it's not good, at home, the way he feels now. It's as if he's given up. I could get a divorce, I suppose. But he is the father of my children. And I still love him. So that's not an option. But, ambitious as I am, I never figured it would end up like this."

That same summer week in 1994, I see an item in the *New York*

Times that in the last five years there has been a significant drop in income—nearly 20 percent—of college-educated white American men. Not minority, high school-educated, or blue-collar, but white management men, the masters of the universe. And it is hitting mainly men in their forties. No such decline is taking place among women. Of course, women, on the whole, are still not making as much money as men. But more women are coming out of professional programs into management jobs. And the service jobs, which most women hold, are the kind of jobs on the increase in our economy, not being downsized like the blue-collar jobs and layers of middle management. These service jobs, I later learn, are now being contracted out, out-sourced, put on a temporary or contingency basis, without benefits or job security. Nevertheless, in new national studies women report they are now carrying some 50 percent of the income burden in some 50 percent of U.S. families.

Downsizing had not yet hit the headlines; in the 1994 elections "the angry white male" had not yet surfaced. But my inner Geiger counter began to click, the way it does when something really foreign to definition, expectation, accepted truth, happens. I trust that click now. It set me on the search that led to the concept of "the feminine mystique," which led to the women's movement for equality. And now, though my thinking and life in the thirty years since—and many other women's—have been conducted within that liberating frame of reference, I feel again a sense of urgent change required. With all the reservations, mistakes, omissions, and downright objections my own feminism has surmounted these years, its liberating force for women, for our whole society, has always prevailed. But my inner Geiger counter does not lie. What I sense here is something basic, something that cannot be evaded or handled at all in the usual feminist terms.

What I sense is the need for a paradigm shift beyond feminism, beyond sexual politics, beyond identity politics altogether. A new paradigm for women and men. Since then, the more I've thought about this—and begun to try and make it happen—the more I realize a lot of other people from very different groups and political persuasions than mine are moving in the same direction. There's a mounting sense that the crises we are now facing, or denying, cannot be solved in the same terms we use to conduct our personal or political or business or family lives. They can no longer be seen in terms of gender. The old paradigm still shaping our thinking may keep us from seeing these problems for what they are, much less solving them.

DEFINING A PARADIGM SHIFT

My son Daniel, who is a theoretical physicist working on superstring theory, gets very cross at the idea of social and political scientists using, or misusing, the term "paradigm shift." "It's not just a change in your worldview," he scolds me. "It's more basic than that. It's a change in the system that defined the problems, the models, and the methods on which a whole community of scientists was trained, and which led to real advance in knowledge. It's when that system no longer works in reality that a paradigm shift has to occur."

"Exactly," I tell him. "That's what's happening now. In feminism and other places."

In the 1960s, I came across Thomas S. Kuhn's *The Structure of Scientific Revolutions.* It elucidated the concept of paradigm shift and caused a great controversy in the scientific community around the time my own *The Feminine Mystique* came out in 1963. When I read Kuhn's book, I realized that breaking through that age-old definition of woman only in sexual relation to man—wife, mother, sex object, housewife—never as a person defining herself by her own actions in society, was, in fact, a paradigm shift. The *personhood of woman* makes the whole gestalt different. It defines a different set of problems from the old "woman problem"—as the experts and the women's magazines kept calling it back then—"Why are American women so frustrated in their role as women? Maybe they've had too much education, etc., etc." After the paradigm shift, the problem became: what keeps American women from moving, participating, as full equals in every area of American society?

Paradigm shift, as Kuhn articulated it, happens when a system that seemed to work perfectly well (like a science predicated on planets circling around the earth before Copernicus or the physics of light before Newton and Einstein) begins to confront problems that even the most brilliant researchers cannot solve in the old terms or even the most fine-tuned tools can no longer measure. Anomalies, in fact, may have shown up for years, but nobody paid any attention to them until a crisis occurred that might not have been apparent to many still caught up in the old paradigm. Some scientists saw the crisis and realized it could not be solved by stretching the old box. It just didn't fit. Little alterations wouldn't work.

Scientists immersed in the crisis, but not so caught up in the center of the old paradigm, might suddenly, as if in the middle of the night, find a new way to look at the whole system. And if that led to new solutions in reality, opening up the science again, it would become the new paradigm, though not without a lot of controversy and opposition from those with vested interests in the old paradigm. But the paradigm shift, required for the evolution of the science and the evolution of knowledge, would not mean discarding the old paradigm, which, after all, had led to the evolution up to this point. Most of it, the concrete accomplishments, would be incorporated in the new paradigm.

So light was seen as material corpuscles before Newton, then as waves, and, after Einstein, photons—quantum mechanical entities that exhibit some of the characteristics of waves and some of particles. Before Einstein, Kuhn said, "what had previously been meant by space was necessarily flat, homogeneous, isotropic, and unaffected by the presence of matter. To make the transition to Einstein's universe the whole conceptual web whose strands are space, time, matter, force, and so on had to be shifted and laid down again on nature whole."

MEANING FOR THE WOMEN'S MOVEMENT

Before the modern women's movement, all our maps in every field were defined by men, and women were defined in relation to men. It was a paradigm shift when we began to challenge the rubrics of theory and practice that in every field had been developed only from male experience. This paradigm shift opened up every field, as women began to move in great numbers through the 1960s and 1970s and 1980s into law and medicine, all the sciences, business, art, politics, the humanities. "It changed my life," women of three generations still stop me in the street, restaurant, or airport to say. It opened life, personal and political, family and professional, in complex new directions.

But today I look back and admit anomalies that kept making me try and stretch the box of feminism long before this crisis. For me, the unwritten, inviolable law against which any and all thinking about women must be tested is simply life itself. Does it open or close real life as women live it? Does it permit more choice, autonomy, freedom, control over their lives? Does it empower or restrict?

In fact, that's where I came in, in the 1950s, after I was fired from a newspaper job for being pregnant with my second child and retreated guiltily to the life of a suburban housewife in a beautiful old Victorian house in Rockland County, New York. In those days, a wife and mother who worked outside the home was supposed to be losing her femininity, undermining her husband's masculinity, and neglecting her children no matter how much her paycheck was needed to help pay the bills.

For those of us who started the modern women's movement— mothers, housewives, volunteer leaders, and formerly invisible women in corporate and government offices and trade union halls— the paradigm shifted overnight, it seemed. The new paradigm was simply the ethos of American democracy—equality of opportunity, our own voice in the decisions of our destiny—but applied to women in terms of concrete daily life as the theory and practice of democracy may never have been applied before.

And how truly empowering it was, those first actions we took as an organized women's movement, getting Title VII of the Civil Rights Act enforced against sex discrimination. The commissioner of the Equal Opportunity Commission, like the legislators who passed the civil rights bill, treated our campaign against sex discrimination as a joke. They stopped laughing when we began the class-action suits, when the telephone company had to pay millions of dollars in reparations to women who never before had been allowed to apply for jobs beyond operator. How empowering it was when we demanded to be served at the Oak Room of the Plaza Hotel, where men made their business deals and women were excluded. How world-enlarging it was when we used the law to make newspapers stop advertising all the good jobs "Help Wanted Male," and the saleswoman, clerk, waitress, and cleaner jobs "Help Wanted Female." Women began enrolling in great numbers in law schools and medical schools, and M.B.A. and Ph.D. programs. Women went from 8 percent of medical school graduates in 1970 to 34 percent in 1990.

SEXUAL POLITICS, IDENTITY POLITICS

For younger women, coming from the student movement of the 1960s and without much experience yet of the life most women led, the paradigm came from a different place, sexual politics: women as a whole sex rising against men as a whole sex. Sexual politics created a model of gender based on class warfare and racial oppression, and I had trouble with it from the beginning because it didn't fit *life*—life as I'd known it, life as other women knew it, even scientific knowledge about life. Sexual politics expressed a lot of rage, rage that had to be suppressed when women were completely dependent on men, or rage taken out on men and children covertly or directed on our own bodies. But did it open women's lives to new growth and development to see women against men, the oppressed against the oppressors, down with men, down with marriage, down with motherhood, down with everything women ever had done to attract men, down with everything men had done in history, the patriarchs, the brutes?

When I left the presidency of the National Organization for Women (NOW) in 1970, sexual politics was already dividing our strength. I helped start the National Women's Political Caucus to organize women in both major parties to "make policy, not coffee." I began putting most of my energy into teaching, lecturing, and writing again—all of it geared to what I saw as the need for feminist thought to evolve.

In *The Second Stage*, published in 1981, I proposed coming to new terms with family, with motherhood, with men, with careers, going beyond the impossible dilemmas of the old paradigm, the male model or its sexual obverse. My views were bitterly attacked by *Ms.* and other voices of what was becoming "politically correct" feminism, as if I was betraying the women's movement. I was deeply hurt by those attacks but had no desire to mount a divisive counterfeminist movement. In my writing, I took on a new frontier instead, the denial of age defined only as programmed deterioration from youth to terminal senility.

I bowed out of feminist organizational politics altogether, except when asked for help. In California I was doing research at the Andrus Center for Gerontology at the University of Southern California for my book *The Fountain of Age*. The faculty of the U.S.C. Study of Women and Men in Society, as they called it, did ask for my help in enlisting the newly powerful women in the film industry and in Los Angeles political and civil life in support of women's studies.

I saw the chance to bring women who had become empowered in the larger society together with women's studies theorists and other academics, perhaps to help feminist thought evolve beyond the abstract rhetoric of sexual politics. Our "think tank," as we called it, did just that. It included professors of law, science, history, and women's studies, as well as film stars, directors and executives, Los Angeles political leaders, women judges and entrepreneurs, rabbis, and church women.

In the 1980s in cities like Boston, New York, Los Angeles, and San Francisco where feminist consciousness was supposedly at the cutting edge, women of childbearing years were dividing into bitter antagonistic camps as they were forced into no-win, either-or choices, motherhood versus career. I saw no real equality unless women could "have it all" as men can. But they can't do it exactly as men do, can they, as long as women are the ones who give birth to children, and still take, or are supposed to take, most of the responsibility for raising them?

All through the 1980s, the women's movement for equality spread throughout society, as women in great numbers were moving out of law school, medical school, M.B.A. programs, and community colleges into jobs and professions. Women were using affirmative action to get skilled trade jobs; they were seeking leadership positions in unions and professional organizations. Women's legal and policy advocacy groups grew, and African American, Asian, and Latina women, women sociologists and scientists, Catholic nuns, and Jewish rabbis formed their own caucuses. And, following the "baby bust," in those years when women were liberating themselves from the feminine mystique, many chose to have babies in their thirties and forties.

Yet polls began to appear showing younger women not wanting to call themselves feminists, though they seemed to identify with every item of the women's agenda of equality. During the Reagan years, a backlash was growing, pushed by the religious right; in the media, there were cover stories of gray-suited career women putting down briefcases, picking up babies and putting on aprons. A law providing unpaid parental leave couldn't even get through Congress.

"Identity politics," they started calling it inside the Washington beltway. "Special interests," the politicians and the pundits were calling the women, the blacks, the gays, the workers, the handicapped, the Latinos. The people whom the government and laws of our democracy were supposed to protect from the otherwise overwhelming tyranny of corporate power were being labeled "special interests" just like the oil industry or the lumber barons. Surely, women—who are 52 percent of the American people—should never have let ourselves be defined by such a model, based originally on corporate power. Is the strength to put the interests of the people first weakened as we increasingly organize over separate, single issues? Is the vision of the common good clouded if we define our enemy in terms of race or gender or sexual orientation—black versus white, women versus men, gay versus straight?

The energy of the leading feminist organizations has been focused on abortion or on sexual politics—rape, date rape, pornography. The work of the religious right and other far right groups led to the bombing of abortion clinics and a "gag rule" prohibiting hospitals or clinics receiving federal funds from giving women any information about abortion possibilities. There is no question in my mind that the far right has focused on abortion as symbol and substance of woman's independence, autonomy, control over her own body, and destiny. But were we somehow letting those who opposed all our rights, our very personhood as women, box us in, confine us, and define the terms of our unfinished battle too narrowly? Year after year we spent all our organizational energy and funds fighting for the right to abortion, the battle we had already won in Congress and the courts and public opinion.

Ought not at least as much energy go into breaking down the remaining barriers to women's earning and advancing in our economy to equality with men? Key to that, in the United States, would be to change the structures that make it very difficult for American women to combine childbearing and advancing in business and the professions. I discovered that the countries where women's earnings were virtually equal to men—Australia, for instance—were those with strong national policies on child care, parental leave, and flexible hours.

At a Rockefeller retreat on Cape Cod, I joined Marian Wright Edelman of the Children's Defense Fund and my long time women's movement colleagues Kathy Bonk, Diana Meehan, and a few others to consider enlarging the definition of choice. We proposed adding the "choice to have children," demanding policies in the workplace, schools, and other institutions that take into account the realities of combining work and family, for women and men. But other feminists, those leading the battle on abortion and some at the U.S.C. think tank, did not want to broaden choice in this way. "All our lives we were told to put children and the family first. Our movement has to put women first."

BACKLASH AT THE LOCAL LEVEL

I objected to this kind of "political correctness." Women don't always put women first. By mutual consent, our think tank at U.S.C. moved from the faculty of the Study of Women and Men in Society to the Warren Bennis Leadership Institute at the U.S.C. School of Business. My last spring at U.S.C., I was lecturing the executive M.B.A. students on women's experience and management. I assumed these sophisticated young men and women (about 60 percent white male, the rest women and minorities) sent by their companies as candidates for top management would take for granted ideas about "equality" and "diversity" that at least got lip service in academia and industry. It was an all-afternoon Saturday session. These students in mid-career worked during the week. An hour in, I couldn't ignore a growing sense of hostility as I recounted how women had moved from the invisible industry of housework to their present state. I'd not felt such an aura of disdain since the early days of the women's movement.

I stopped my lecture, gave them a ten-minute break, and when they came back, said I wanted to talk about the hostility they seemed to feel at the whole idea of equality for women and blacks. I didn't expect this anymore from bright, young, would-be managers in corporate America, which had begun to see "diversity" in bottom-line terms. Could they be secretly afraid that by the time they got their M.B.A.s those on-the-way-to-the-top management jobs they were being groomed for might not be there, the way California companies were downsizing? There was a tense silence, then one twenty-thirty-something jock stood up to say: "You may be right. But I'll tell you one thing, if my job is gone, and I have to start hunting, there won't be an even playing field. The woman or the black will get the job."

It did no good to explain, even with statistics, that the jobs white men were losing were not being taken by women and minorities. They were the casualties of corporate downsizing done strictly for short-term profit—stock market reasons. The women and blacks were easier, more convenient, more comfortable scapegoats.

Our empowerment as women became visible politically after

Anita Hill in the summer of 1991 blew the whistle on Supreme Court nominee Clarence Thomas over sexual harassment. The Senate confirmed him nevertheless. In 1992, women voters, turning out in unprecedented numbers, elected unprecedented numbers of women to Congress and put Bill Clinton into the White House. One of his first acts was the elimination of the "gag rule" preventing family planning counselors from giving any information on abortion. He also signed into law a parental leave bill. In 1993, he appointed and the Senate overwhelmingly confirmed Ruth Bader Ginsburg for the Supreme Court despite her unequivocal stand in favor of abortion rights.

At about this time funds were raised to take a poll that truly crossed lines of race, class, and generations to find out the concerns of women in the 1990s. The poll, conducted and released as "Women's Voices" by the Center for Policy Alternatives and the Ms. Foundation, showed, to the amazement of the politically correct, that none of the sexual issues, including abortion, was among the main problems concerning women today, young or old, black or white. They were for choice, overwhelmingly. But the percentages ranking any of the sexual issues—rape, date rape, sexual harassment, pornography, abortion—as of major concern were very small.

For the great majority of women, according to the poll, the main problems were jobs—how to get them, how to keep them, how to get ahead in them—meeting the responsibilities of children and career, and living the equality we'd fought for. The economy itself was based on the two-paycheck family. Women constituted nearly 50 percent of the work force. And in some new studies in 50 percent of families, women earned 50 percent or more of the family income.

My sense of crisis came in the summer of 1994, as I prepared to come to Washington as a guest scholar at the Woodrow Wilson International Center for Scholars. Having finally finished *The Fountain of Age*, I decided to write my memoirs. Packing up my papers, I did a double-take at a number of random items I'd been clipping from the business pages of newspapers.

Male, Educated, and in a Pay Bind
(*New York Times*, Feb. 11, 1994)

For the first time since World War II, college-educated men in their late 40s and early 50s—normally the prime earning years—are suffering a steep decline in wages, finally getting caught in the downward mobility that has hit most other groups of male workers.

By comparison, the million or so college-educated women in this age group have seen their median incomes, adjusted for inflation, rise slightly since 1988. But at $25,818, the median is still well below that of their male peers, although for many households, the women's earnings cushion the men's losses.

The War Between the Sexes
(*The Economist*, March 5, 1994)

Women have been the job market's big success story in the past two decades. But as they have found jobs, men have lost them. Have [women] driven men from the workplace . . . ?

WHAT TO DO?

Now I see the impossible paradox for women: *women are achieving what begins to look like equality because the men are doing worse.* Is their loss really our gain?

Women are benefitting from the changes in the economy, with more control over their lives than their mothers ever dreamed of. The great majority work at jobs that may not be the greatest but give them a life in their forties and fifties, after their kids are off, though the juggling of children and job in their thirties is tough. Many women are doing as well or better than those downsized men.

Studying the pattern in these news items, I sense a backlash much more serious than the drum-beating loin-cloth-wearing masculine impersonators who follow Robert Bly, author of "Iron: A Book About Men." I notice the new custody decisions, in Michigan and California, where women lose custody of a child because they have a demanding job or are getting their law degree or Ph.D. and have the child part of the day in day care. The father's new wife, or mother, will stay home all day with the child. And the "family values" cry is being spread by the religious right, even as its zealots continue to bomb abortion clinics. Feminist groups are mobilizing to defend abortion clinics. But who is mobilizing to confront the economic inequality and dislocation threatening the survival and stability of families far more than is abortion or pornography?

In our thinking about women, I see there has to be a paradigm shift, not just from sexual politics (though the increased violence against women and abuse of children may be a symptom of the rage of men dispossessed of their dominance) but from the whole focus on our status vis-à-vis man. If women are winning, and men are losing now, how long can we really win? The fact is, most women still live in some kind of family with men, and they will subtly suffer—economically and emotionally—if the downsizing and insecurity of the men continue. We must face the real economic threat to family values.

As for women alone, single parents, lesbian couples, the politics of hate that is rising from and stirring up the rage of the threatened men will surely turn on them. I hear that Rush Limbaugh calls me a feminazi. If "jobs" and "work and family" are what concern women most now, we have to mobilize to protect our children, our families, ourselves in a new coalition with men. Should the women's attitude be "up with women, forget the men"? The scapegoating of women is not the only danger. I see virulent intergenerational warfare pitting the youthful Generation X against the grandparents on Social Security, Medicare, and Medicaid.

Economy Bites the Edge Off Generation X
(Los Angeles Times, Feb. 24, 1994)

Is it fair to tax 20-somethings to pay Social Security and Medicaid for their great-grandparents . . . ? With thousands of dollars in student loans to pay back, Generation X-ers seek to avoid a lifetime of "McJobs" all the while cursing their grandparents for mortgaging their future with debt.

Nobody elects me, but I decide to use my berth at the Woodrow Wilson Center to organize the New Paradigm Seminar for policy makers to look beyond identity politics and toward a new paradigm of women, men, and community. I call some new leaders of women's organizations I have come to respect, and also men and women from the AFL-CIO, American Association of Retired Persons (AARP), Brookings Institution, and the Urban Institute, economists and political scientists, to attempt a new kind of thinking about the economic problems basic to our lives—problems that can no longer be seen in terms of women alone, or women versus men.

My first call is to Heidi Hartmann, who has just won a MacArthur Fellow award for her economic work on women's lives. I'm no economist, but I learned economics in the field, as it were, working for labor union newspapers when I first got out of college. It only struck me after I wrote *The Feminine Mystique* and became a feminist how little formal, traditional economics or even radical, Marxist economics had to do with women's lives or putting a value on women's work, even calling it "labor." Heidi agrees to cochair the new paradigm seminar with me. She is not only a brilliant economist but a Washington insider as I am not. She, too, is concerned that feminist organizations are not giving priority to economic issues—wages, jobs, attacks on welfare and affirmative action—in their preoccupation with abortion and sexual issues. A cheerful no-nonsense woman with several kids, she is using her MacArthur award to enlarge her small house and put the Institute for Women's Policy Research which she founded and directs on the map.

Anne Bryant of the American Association of University Women, Cindy Marano of Wider Opportunities for Women, and other leaders of mainstream women's organizations seem eager to participate. Susan Bianchi-Sand, former head of the flight attendants' union also will attend. Under the banner of the Council of Presidents of 110 women's organizations, she has begun to organize a countervailing feminist force—with others from Black Women United for Action to the Junior League to the YWCA—who want to focus much of their energies and resources on jobs and life's economic realities.

I go to see Lane Kirkland, then head of the AFL-CIO whom I had met before and who had been helpful when I was working on *The Fountain of Age*. He does not discourage me. He tells me to invite some of the key union leaders and sends his own research director. He tells me of the strike in Flint, Michigan, where after General Motors downsized 10,000 workers, those left are working seventy- and eighty-hour weeks. They complain of too little time to spend with their families.

I visit Horace Deets and his colleagues at the AARP. They tell me that their members over the age of fifty are the hardest hit by downsizing. In great majority, they want to keep on working, are the most experienced, best paid, but the first to be laid off.

My old friends Amitai Etzioni, head of the Communitarian movement, and Seymour Martin Lipset, Hazel Professor of Public Policy and Sociology at George Mason University and senior fellow at the Woodrow Wilson Center, urge me on. I receive many names of people to invite—a disparate stew of economists and policy makers, not just women, not just the usual feminist suspects.

A campaign for a shorter workweek, a half century after the battle for the forty-hour workweek in the Roosevelt era, might be one alternative to downsizing, not only keeping more men and women on the job, but relieving some of the work-family stress in the child-bearing years. It also might enable the young and not so young to combine education and work on a life-time basis and keep older people from being pushed out as they are now, not only in their sixties, but fifties and forties. These and other ideas build momentum for the new paradigm seminar in the fall of 1994.

2

DOWNSIZING: WOMEN, MEN, TIME, MONEY

The small library of the Woodrow Wilson Center is a distinguished, intimate space. I ask them to take the big table out so we can sit more or less in a circle. We are a distinguished peer group of thinkers—academics, policy makers, activists, managers, labor leaders. Though I ask a few to "present" at the beginning of each session, we proceed in an ongoing dialogue.

It's become clear to me, I tell them, that the basic economic problems that we confront today can't be met by some of the strategies that have worked in the past or by "identity politics" altogether. You break through sexism and provide more jobs for women, but now jobs altogether are being downsized. You break through age discrimination and enforce a law so that people are not turned out of jobs because of age, and now their jobs are being eliminated. There has to be some new consensus, a new community transcending the polarization, to confront basic structural questions.

There is a critical mass of people here in Washington that can raise new questions. Can we say, "Keep the women and fire the men" and ignore the backlash against women? We certainly cannot countenance the danger to women's empowerment if women don't have jobs. Can we say, "Keep on the people who are over forty and don't hire the young," and ignore the intergenerational warfare? Is the recent feminist focus on abortion rights attacks, violence against women, sexual harassment, and rape a focus on symptoms of an even greater threat to women's empowerment—the economic threat from the jobs crisis confronting men and women?

We've known about the effect of downsizing and structural changes in the workplace for the high school-educated, less than high school-educated, and blue-collar workers, but it's time to realize that white, college-educated, middle management men in their forties and older have had nearly a 20 percent drop in income between 1986 through 1992 according to data collected by the Census Bureau.

While the income of white males has been dropping, women's income has continued to rise almost imperceptibly, although still not up to men's levels. Yet women are not taking jobs away from men. The jobs that men have had, both blue collar and middle management, are being eliminated. Women's jobs, service jobs, and jobs in the health and helping professions are generally not being eliminated. So women are not suffering the immediate actuality of the job downsizing as much as men, though a lot of women married to the men are caught in the anxiety.

The increasing generational polarization feeds the anxiety. Generation X is saying "We're paying all this Social Security we're never going to collect ourselves. We don't get the good job offers the baby boomers got when they came out of college." You were supposed to be promoted up and up and up until you were sixty and now you're forty and suddenly it isn't happening. No matter how many figures you release saying that there's a lot of new jobs that pay more than average, a lot of people aren't getting those jobs. The downsizing is a fact of life that creates enormous anxiety and rage out there.

Might this not be the time for a shorter workweek as an alternative to downsizing? This would meet the needs of women and men in the childrearing years and people throughout life as they continue further training, education, and work. This would help older people who shouldn't be pushed out altogether and who would welcome a less rigid schedule. Could it also meet the needs of employers who prefer today to hire temporary or part-time workers if we fight to have such work covered by pro-rated benefits?

We have to have new thinking about competitiveness, new thinking about the bottom line, new thinking about benefits, new thinking about work in terms of time and family, and new definitions of success if we are going to build a new paradigm.

NEGATIVE EQUITY

Heidi Hartmann, from her command of income and economic statistics, gives further evidence of the need for a new paradigm:

Men's labor force participation is declining, while women's labor force participation continues to increase. It looks like the participation rates are going to meet in the middle and that is frightening to some people. In fact, this makes a lot of sense—a different way our economy could be, a model in which women's and men's lives look more alike economically, where both women and men are working to support families and both are doing household work. The new norm of the family is one in which both the husband and wife work. As seen in Table 2-1.1, by 1992 46 percent of all married couple families had a husband and wife in the labor force, up from one-third of families in 1972. This means that both husband and wife were earners in 59 percent of married couples.

The positive side of women's movement into the labor force is their ability to earn income, to support themselves. Women have more ability to make decisions about their own lives. Over time, even women who have families alone are less likely to be poor than they were thirty years ago.

The rest of the success story is the new kinds of jobs women have gone into. Women have been working in the sectors of the economy that have been growing: education, the public sector, health, etc. Despite all the downsizing that's in the news, we still saw a tremendous increase of women managers in those industries. The growth

TABLE 2.1 WOMEN AND FAMILY INCOME

Table 2-1.1 Distribution of Family Types

	Married Couple Families			Single-Headed Families			All Families
Year	Total	Wife in Paid Labor Force	Wife Not in Paid Labor Force	Total	Male–Headed	Female-Headed	
1973	85.0%	35.4%	49.7%	15.0%	2.6%	12.4%	100%
1992	77.8%	46.0%	31.8%	22.2%	4.5%	17.7%	100%

Note: Economic Policy Institute analysis of Census Bureau data.

Table 2-1.2 Shares of Family Income Going to Various Income Groups

Year	Lowest Fifth	Second Fifth	Third Fifth	Fourth Fifth	Top Fifth	Average
1973	5.5%	11.9%	17.5%	24.0%	41.1%	100.0%
1992	4.3%	10.5%	16.5%	24.0%	44.7%	100.0%

Note: Economic Policy Instutute analysis of Census Bureau data.

Table 2-1.3 Husbands' and Wives' Hours of Work (Annual Hours)—Married-couple Families with Children

Year	Lowest Fifth	Second Fifth	Third Fifth	Fourth Fifth	Top Fifth	Average
Employed Husbands						
1979	1,996	2,180	2,224	2,273	2,372	2,211
1989	1,958	2,207	2,239	2,299	2,428	2,234
Percent Change	-1.9%	1.2%	0.7%	1.1%	2.4%	1.0%
Employed Wives						
1979	1,001	1,226	1,314	1,478	1,567	1,347
1989	1,181	1,414	1,554	1,624	1,694	1,516
Percent Change	18.0%	15.0%	18.0%	10.0%	8.0%	13.0%

Note: Joint Economic Committee analysis of the Panel Study of Income Dynamics.

Source: Compiled by the Institute for Women's Policy Research from Tables 1.5, 1.6, and 1.25 in Lawrence Mishel and Jared Bernstein, *The State of Working America, 1994–95*, Economic Policy Institute Series (New York: M.E. Sharpe, 1994).

in the number of women managers is greater than the growth in the number of male managers.

At the same time there is greater inequality now between the top and the bottom of families. Between 1973 and 1992, three-fifths of the families with the lowest incomes actually lost income in real terms. Only the top fifth of the families already earning the most money gained substantially (See Table 2-1.2). It is actually women's work that has kept some of the middle from falling further. Women have increased their hours of work by 13 percent and men by only 1 percent (See Table 2-1.3). In the lowest fifth of families men actually decreased their hours by 2 percent. Women's contribution to family income has increased as well (See Figure 2-1).

The wage gap between women and men is closing. If they work year-round, full time, women now earn 72 percent of what men earn, compared with 60 percent in the 1980s. Women are doing better than men in part because men are doing worse. That, according to Roberta Spalter-Roth at the Institute for Women's Policy Re-

FIGURE 2.1   WORKING WIVES' CONTRIBUTIONS TO FAMILY INCOME, 1970–1992

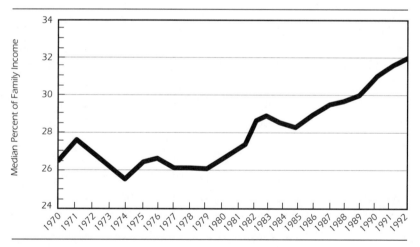

Source: Institute for Women's Policy Research, based on Current Population Survey data in Howard V. Hayghe, "Working Wives' Contributions to Family Incomes," *Monthly Labor Review* 116, no.8 (1993): 42.

search, is "negative equity." The women's movement wanted more equity, but "maybe we don't want it at the price of negative equity."

Some of the feminist leaders keep slipping back into the singular focus on women. Economist Barbara Bergman of American University says:

There's bound to be, among some men, a resentment about women's advancement. We should have better unemployment insurance and better retraining to take care of some of the casualties. But part of the reason that men's earnings are dropping is that there used to be a universal premium for maleness and not all employers want to pay that anymore. We wish that we would all rise, but don't knock equality.

Equality is very important. We can devote part of our energy as feminists to things that help both men and women such as national health insurance and getting the workweek down, but we can't devote even a large part of our energy to things which are sex neutral. We have to keep our energy on things that specifically help women even though there's a backlash. If there's a backlash, that shows we're making progress.

Some of the men present are turned off by these ideas as, I suppose, some of the feminists are made uneasy by the fact that I really mean a new paradigm for women and men. Does this mean a betrayal or abandonment of feminism? Or do we have to move to this new paradigm in order to keep advancing? Henry Aaron, distinguished economist from the Brookings Institution, sees it in less either/or terms:

I'm not sure there's anything wrong with what you're calling "negative equity." It's the likely consequence of equalization in our economy within which productivity over all isn't growing. As women are making increasing commitments to jobs and discriminatory practices are diminishing, although not removed, their earnings have been closing the gap with the average male earnings. If the overall total isn't growing, it is likely that average male earnings will decline. That suggests there is a feminist stake in overall productivity growth precisely because it would reduce the kinds of obstacles (backlash) arising from male reactions to diminished earnings.

My idea of a shorter workweek and more flexible work structures as an alternative to downsizing makes some of my feminist sisters uneasy. Diana Pearce, who heads the Women in Poverty Project at Wider Opportunities for Women in Washington, D.C., says:

We devalue people when they work fewer hours. On the one hand, people want flexibility, but on the other hand, if you take part-time work you're denigrated in lots of ways. Most part-time workers in all but two states are not covered by unemployment insurance no matter how many hours they work. Part-time workers are disproportionately women. We assume they want to spend more time with the family so they'll take everything else that goes with that package—no benefits, the insecurity, no growth on the job. That's not true.

The question of "competitiveness" is raised in the context of the global economy. A Woodrow Wilson Center Fellow and Brookings Institution Guest Scholar, Patricia Springborg of the University of Sydney, Australia, points out that "it's an economic deterrent to hire full-time workers if you get a free ride on benefits with part-time. Yet in countries worldwide that provide to part-time workers benefits equal with those of full-time workers, there is still a trend toward part-time work over full-time work."

The idea that you can't be a working mother and do justice to your kids is growing in America, and there are reports of studies showing that men whose wives don't work do better. The backlash that's worrying me is whether women will begin to be discriminated against in a new way. If there aren't some basic changes in our economy that go beyond women's equity—women could lose the jobs that are their real empowerment.

But we can't see any real solutions, locked as I think we all still are in the either/or, no-wins of the old paradigm. The whole idea of greater flexibility, shorter work time—which a lot of women and men seem to want and, for different reasons, employers in our changing economy are introducing—makes the women especially uneasy, since it would inevitably mean lower wages, wouldn't it?

We don't even want to talk about flexibility if it means reducing wages. Too many women and families are dependent on earnings. But more and more women, and men too, are working involuntarily at temporary or part-time jobs without benefits. Nobody is proposing we give up the battle for equality. What's worrying me is that we're going to be pushed back in the battle for equality. We get locked into our rhetoric while reality is changing around us. For others, overwork is a problem. The following two clips from my file emphasize these trends:

Low Pay and Closed Doors Greet Young in Job Market
(New York Times, March 10, 1994)

Once-reliable employers like T.W.A. and Sears have dumped workers, and executives with masters degrees remain as vulnerable as production line assemblers. . . . Temporary jobs are at their highest levels ever. There are 24.4 million part-time and temporary workers. . . . "

Overwork Overwhelms Families of the `90s
(Boston Globe, Oct. 6, 1994)

In some reverse of labor history, the working class of today—upper, middle, lower working class, which is to say nearly everyone—works longer hours than most of our parents. We seem to be evolving into two classes, the underemployed and the overemployed, those who are desperate for work and those who are desperate for time. Especially family time.

. . . In manufacturing jobs, the average workweek is now some 41 hours, higher than at any time since World War II. That includes a substantial portion of workers for whom eight and ten hours of overtime have become routine.

In the white-collar world the average workweek is now just under 44 hours. Among executives it's 46.5 hours. Among male executives it's 48.2 hours. In every workplace that's been downsized and sped up, in every office where workers are doing three jobs for the price of two, in every office where the CEO brags that "productivity" is up, the workload is going up and up.

Employers have learned that it's cheaper to pay fewer people more money than to hire more people and pay benefits. Workers have learned that those who say "no" may be the next to go. . . . Just last month, a US Air flight attendant with a husband at work, a babysitter going out the door and a 6-year-old in bed with chicken pox was ordered to take a late overtime flight away from home. For arguing with the scheduler, she was fired."

THE CATACLYSMIC ELECTION OF 1994

The new paradigm seminar is not surprised by the "angry white male" backlash that throws Democrats out of Congress in unprecedented numbers in the election of November 1994—nor by the anxious women who don't vote. Some of us had tried to warn people around the White House and the Democratic Party that women's concerns weren't being reached. We were told we were "off message."

As it turned out, if the women who had elected Clinton in 1992 had come out to vote in '94, a lot of the Republicans whose "Contract with America" would reverse the social welfare policies that have protected women and men since Roosevelt's days would not have been elected. Pollster Celinda Lake shows our informal women's lunch group polling data that indicated it was mainly *married women*, housewives, and women without college graduate degrees, who did not come out to vote in 1994 as they had in 1992. Were these the women whose husbands had been hit by downsizing, perhaps, or the ones harassed now by the burden of carrying the family on those insecure temporary jobs?

Shortly before the 1994 elections, I take part in a forum with representatives of the American Management Association and other corporate executives as well as Secretary of Labor Robert Reich that asked "Is Downsizing Crippling or Strengthening America?" What surprises me are the figures cited by Eric Greenberg, director of management studies for the American Management Association, that show most of the downsizing that "has now become operating procedure for corporate America" is not in response to actual, or anticipated, business downturns or national economic conditions. Nor even is most of it necessary because of technological changes or global competition. The effect on the workers laid off or the morale of those overworked and insecure who are kept on is not mentioned. But profits are increased and, above all, the stock market value goes up in the next quarter.

The rage of these angry white males is vividly expressed at the AMA forum by G.J. Meyers, who relives his own downsizing in a recently published book *Executive Blues: Down and Out in Corporate America.* He had been first downsized as vice president at McDonnell Douglas Corporation, then as vice president for a multinational manufacturing corporation with sales of more than $5 billion a year. Out of work for the first time in his life, he follows every lead, doesn't even get interviews anymore: "I'm jealous of anybody who still has the kind of job I used to have, of almost anybody who has a job, period. My envy of the people who put me here and are still drawing their gigantic pension points is as murderous as my resentment."

Secretary Reich talks about what the growth of the "anxious class" is doing to the American economy and American competitiveness. In the long run, do the overworked, insecure managers and technical workers left identify with the company enough to make the innovations that will keep it competitive in the world market, he asks? I am the only woman on the panel. I ask what all this downsizing is doing to American families—women, children, and men.

This clip from my file describes the negative effects of downsizing in Connecticut:

State's Quality of Life Has Dropped Sharply in Last Ten Years, a Study Finds
(New York Times, Dec. 5, 1994)

The social well-being of Connecticut declined sharply from 1988 on as jobs deteriorated, according to the first study of a state by a new Index of Social Health, innovated by Fordham's Institute for Social Policy.

From 1988 on, not only were more people in Connecticut unemployed but more were out of work for longer periods. . . . The strains on family income during that time were accompanied by a sharp increase in reports of child abuse and of crime, mirroring similar increases across the country.

When the new paradigm seminar participants get together again after that cataclysmic 1994 election, the vulnerability of women— older people, blacks, gays, and other minorities—to that rage growing among "angry white men" and "ambivalent" white women seems clearer. We study a *Wall Street Journal* series, in December 1994, on the new "Great Divides" in America's political culture— the have-more, glass-tower people and the have-lesses. Women, it seems, also divide on those lines. According to the last article in the series, December 14:

The glass-tower people are generally college-educated, economically ascendant, and comfortable with cultural diversity and change. . . . But the have-lesses are generally undereducated, trapped in unrewarding, and sometimes dead-end jobs. . . . They constitute a beleaguered subculture: un-chic, un-minority, and in their opinion, unheard. Liberals, they believe, seem able to muster sympathy for every group—feminists, gays, welfare mothers—except theirs. White homemakers, however, differed sharply from career women. . . . Many women, like men, feel "forgotten," says Mr. Newhouse [Republican pollster]. As they see it, "affirmative action is helping minorities and the rich are getting richer," but nobody is looking out for them.

. . . Reading the election results, Labor Secretary Robert Reich concluded that the nation had just witnessed "the revolt of the anxious class." He explained in a post-election address: "We are on the way to becoming a two-tiered middle class composed of a few winners and a larger group left behind, whose anger and disillusionment is easily manipulated. Today the targets of rage are immigrants, welfare mothers, government officials, gays, and an ill-defined 'counter-culture.' As the middle class continues to erode, who will be the targets tomorrow?"

VIEWS FROM THE AARP

At the new paradigm seminar, Clare Hushbeck of the American Association of Retired Persons (AARP) describes how many people have decided to become "retired" because they haven't been able to find a job. The problem facing AARP is how to promote employment of older people and flexible work arrangements yet not legitimize contingency work that's involuntary. She reports to us:

Midlife and older workers have been disproportionately hit by the waves of downsizing over the last decade. We did a survey in the spring of 1994 asking if our members had been squeezed, nudged, pushed, or shoved out the door. We had anticipated around 1,000 to 1,500 respondents, but we have had 10,000 plus, many with detailed heartrending letters attached.

The majority of these people are white males in their fifties who have been nudged out, or worse, from middle management or professional jobs where they'd been for a number of years and were earning good money. Of those who had found work—and that was only about half of them—80 percent found work only at lower pay, in some cases considerably lower. Sometimes the pay was only 40 percent of what they had been earning previously. There's a great deal of pain out there.

We're pursuing some pretty short-sighted policies, particularly in light of the fact that people are living longer and they're living healthier. The likely trend in pensions and in Social Security is less generosity in the future. The retirement age for Social Security purposes has already increased and is going to go up further. So what is it, exactly, that we expect people to do with the last third of their lives? Some people might like to get in a Winnebago for all of that time, but many people are not going to be able to afford that. This is particularly true for people who've been contingent workers most of their lives. They've never accumulated pension credits and often didn't even have an employer contributing to Social Security on their behalf.

The buzz word has become "training." We need to be training

people to make smoother transitions from one occupation to an-
other or one technology to another. . . . For the longer run, how do we
expect to have any kind of cohesiveness as a society when we have
this growing gap between the haves and the have-nots in terms of
both income, and more recently, employment. We have the overem-
ployed people who are begging for relief—flexible hours, family
leave—and we have underemployed and unemployed people who
are desperate for any job they can get.

UAW FACTORY WORKERS

In the next session, we bring in Dave Yettaw, president of United
Auto Workers Local 599, to tell us about the unprecedented strike of
General Motors workers against the excessive overtime in the Flint,
Michigan, plant. The strike they had just won forced the company to
hire back many of the 10,000 workers who had been downsized. Yettaw gives a sense of a new militant, visionary kind of union leader,
one who might take labor out of its recent doldrums. He tells us:

The factory I represent is the largest in General Motors Northern
America with 12,000 active UAW members. General Motors in 1978
had a peak of 466,000 jobs, and they are now down to 226,000. They
cut their work force by 240,000 jobs, downsizing. The big three auto
makers largely in the first six months of 1995 worked 85 million
man-hours of overtime. That would create 41,000 full-time jobs for
a year on a forty-hour workweek.

Many of my members are working ten hours a day, six days a
week or six weeks in the course of a month. One member worked
twenty-three double shifts in the month of June. Sadly, the overtime
becomes the cocaine of the auto industry. Workers become addicted
to overtime and it becomes their life style. Because of overtime, we
have auto workers making $100,000 a year. It doesn't take long for
blue collar union members making that kind of money to start
thinking like white collar people who are accustomed to making
$100,000 a year. We are fighting that. We are hammering home the

impact of overtime, not only on the community itself but on the workers as well. We want to cut overtime to lift other people out of poverty and create permanent jobs.

In the city of Flint, 45 percent of the children now live at the poverty level. That gives you an idea of the devastation that overtime can have if you're not sharing jobs. We had horrendous health and safety injuries resulting from this overtime, largely repetitive motion injuries on our machine floors and assembly lines. Overtime also pushes our members into greater damaging accumulative effects of toxic chemical hazards that they're exposed to in the workplace.

AFL-CIO Research Director Sheldon Friedman said that even though the auto industry was in a very strong cyclical upturn, there had been absolutely no new hiring in General Motors since 1985. So the average age of the UAW worker is now forty-seven years old. What the company did to adjust to this massive increase in production was to massively increase overtime. The workers were getting injured because of fatigue from the pressure of all this overtime, and it was having a tremendously bad impact on people's family lives.

Yettaw told us the strike was not something the union leadership organized. About 300 members came out of the factories and demanded a strike vote addressing the pressures on the job:

We had 5,000 members vote yes to strike against speed up, lack of manpower, health safety, and excessive overtime and 1,000 voted no. As a result of our victory, 1,000 are being called back in our Flint area and it's rolling across the country. Our strike probably got back somewhere in the neighborhood of 5,000 jobs in GM in 1995.

Paying the premium wage for overtime, time-and-a-half or double time on weekends, is not a problem for the company because the cost in terms of pension and health care benefits of bringing new members on-line is many times that. GM would rather go the route of overtime premiums. So we're going to agitate to increase the overtime penalty.

Organized labor won the eight-hour day about fifty-eight years ago. Productivity is such in the factories that if you were to reduce the work day by one-tenth of an hour, or six minutes a day each year of the contract, in ten years you would be at a thirty-five hour week. Is that too much to ask to extract six minutes a day per year from our productivity increase to put America on a shorter workweek?

We, as organized labor, do want to see shorter work time, not compressed work time! Not ten-hour days, for four days, because in the next downturn, corporate America will be saying they can't survive if you don't work four days, twelve hours. We discussed adding a third shift option similar to the GM plant in Germany which leans toward a seven-hour day. Oddly enough we're coming back around to conditions similar to those prior to the 1930s. Unions now represent only 11 percent of the private sector labor force. As trade unionists, we don't have far to go to hit bottom. Organized labor was about 7 percent of the labor force in 1890.

In the cities, I believe, we are going to see more strikes. The cities are nearly war zones now. If we don't change the opportunity for work in this country, be it job sharing or shorter work time (not compressed time), society literally is going to come apart at the seams. When that does occur, that's when corporate America will give us a new social contract.

Nancy Mills of the Service Employees' International Union reminds us that the only protection against mandatory overtime in America today is union contracts. "One element of the new paradigm needs to be making it possible for workers to organize again," she argues.

TIME VERSUS MONEY

Now we move into the new paradigm. We can talk about shorter work time—not as a special issue for women, "trading time for money," giving up chances for advancement, "the mommy track." We can talk about the actual experience of companies, organizations, cities, and other countries that have instituted the shorter workweek and flexible work options as alternatives to downsizing or in response to work and family needs.

Juliet Schor, author of *The Overworked American*, comes down from Harvard to discuss the issue of work time. In the last Gallup poll in the July 1994 issue of *Health* magazine, one-third of all respondents said they would take a 20 percent cut in household income if they or their spouse could work fewer hours, she says. Although more corporations are offering flexible work schedules and job sharing, relatively few workers are affected by these new practices. Like Dave Yettaw, she decries the negative effects of compulsory overtime:

Right now the big inequality on time is between the overworked and the underemployed, and the underemployed and the unemployed. Under the current law, employers can require people to work overtime, but they have to pay them more money. Compulsory overtime should be abolished. And we should move from a system of premium pay for overtime to a system of compensated time off. That is, if you work more than your standard hours this week or month, you get paid by time off in the future.

An amended Fair Labor Standards Act should ensure a right to free time, something that we do not have in this country. People should be entitled to move forward in their careers and jobs even if they want to work shorter hours. Right now people are forced to make the choice between career success and time, which there is no economic rationale for. It comes out of the old male model of employment where the job is the first priority. That model came about in a very different time when we had mainly single-earner families. In today's environment we should establish the idea that if people do their job well and meet performance criteria, they should not be penalized for wanting to work short hours. It's reasonable to expect people to make income sacrifices for working less but not career sacrifices.

Heidi Hartmann wants to know if any other countries have a right to free time. She suggests that "the long hours in general is a male club idea and a way of keeping women out." Juliet Schor says in a lot of other countries paid vacation time is sacred. I note that in Germany a recent attempt to shorten vacation time and holiday time in order to keep stores open longer was absolutely refused by the people. Donna Lenhoff of the Women's Legal Defense Fund is skeptical, seeing women in law firms where the forty-hour workweek is the "mommy track," not a partnership track. "It's appalling but the only way to change this situation is to get the men to reduce their hours as well. Yet we are given nothing but economic excuses for not doing that."

Julie Schor insists there is no real economic rationale for longer hours in terms of productivity:

We know that per hour productivity is higher when people work fewer hours. There's also a point beyond which total productivity begins to fall when hours are so high that you begin to get the stress and burnout dimensions. It's the corporate culture that promulgates the idea that long hours are necessary, as long as you can hire other people to make up the hours, it's not a question of productivity.

The final dimension is the benefits package. Benefits are paid on a per person basis, not pro-rated by the hour, so there is a very strong incentive for employers to hire as small a number of people as possible and to work them for as many hours as possible. We need either to get medical insurance out of the enterprise or to pro-rate by the hour.

A lot of men are getting burned out. A lot of men, especially in their forties and fifties, are sick of the eighty-hour weeks, too. There's a piece in the *Wall Street Journal* talking about how corporations are not really allowing, much less encouraging, men to take all the maternity-paternity benefits they are entitled to under the Family and Medical Leave.

Ellen Bravo of 9 to 5, National Association of Working Women and author of *The Job/Family Challenge* is also pessimistic: "There would be a lot more people who would opt for flexible schedules if they didn't get punished in terms of their pay and if benefits were pro-rated. Until men change their practices, women won't be equal, and men won't do that until they stop being punished for it."

Jared Bernstein of the Economic Policy Institute and co-author of *The State of Work in America* advances our thinking:

One of the reasons for this steep increase in labor supply and hours has to do with falling wage rates. Any new paradigm, it seems to me, would have to embrace solutions or ideas about how we reverse this steep wage decline. The only way family income can keep from falling now is for family members to run faster, work longer hours just to stay in place. For women, at least above the median income, hourly pay has been rising, but from the median on down, women's rate of wage loss has been similar to men's. At the median, men's wages are falling more than women's wages are rising. In fact, 75 percent of the closing of the gender gap has to do with men's wages falling, and only 25 percent is accountable by women's wages rising.

We are no longer diverted by "negative equity," women versus men. But how are we going to sell the new paradigm? Sandra Myers of the National Endowment for the Humanities asks this question. "We're getting to know what it is, but all of these reforms, changes, and good ideas need to be explained in a context that says that the new paradigm is not just for the good of women. It's for the good of society. That's very soft talk in a lean and mean world," she notes.

I try to pull it together. Either you can go the route of focusing on what women make compared with men or you can go the route that something has to be done in terms of the whole society and the whole economy. Trying to come to a new paradigm, we have to be very careful that we see it all. For example, you can't talk about a shorter workweek as an alternative to downsizing or removing compulsory overtime without talking about getting pro-rated and portable benefits, and ending discrimination against part-time workers. If a new coalition begins thinking in those terms, then it isn't just for women, just for men, just for minorities, just for older people, it's for everybody, it's a new community. People in our society want a new vision of community.

3

FLEXIBLE WORK OPTIONS IN PERSPECTIVE

We spend several sessions in our new paradigm seminar hearing how organizations, companies, cities, and other countries have, in fact, made a shorter workweek or flexible time, work for the benefit not only of the individual worker but of the "bottom line." Two bankers come in every month from Minneapolis to participate in the seminar. I like the increasing diversity. Participants in different sessions now include a deputy assistant to the president for domestic policy, a special advisor to the under secretary for global affairs at the State Department, a district judge, a senior analyst at the Office of Technology Assessment, the executive director of the National Association of Women Business Owners, a senior policy advisor to the vice president, the public affairs director for the Urban Institute, the director of the Hispanic Association of Colleges, a longtime Republican activist on women's issues, the chief economist for the AFL-CIO, the civil rights director of the Newspaper Guild, a number of economists from the Brookings Institution and other Washington think tanks, and members of the Global Conference Secretariat of the State Department. We hear from several organizations about their experiences with alternative work schedules.

WORKPLACE EXPERIENCES

Anne Bryant, head of the American Association of University Women (AAUW), describes how its staff has gone to a four-day flex week yet maintained the same 37.5 hours of work per week.

Why did we do it? It was the stress; it was the workload. The whole issue of home life was really hitting our work force of 104 people.

First, we undertook a study of all the jobs at AAUW according to the standards we advocate for pay equity on Capitol Hill. Then we set up a system of work teams—grassroots organizing, publication processing, marketing, finance, information systems, programing, and communications. One of the issues with a four-day flex week is who will be there who knows the job when the person who regularly does it is out.

Next, we began a three-month pilot program with a four-day flex week. You could choose to have Monday off or Friday off or remain in the five-day workweek. The exempt staff, as before, often works longer hours, but the difference is that on Friday or Monday, they have a three-day weekend and hopefully can recoup their strength. Unquestionably, morale has greatly increased. Also we have flex hours between 7 and 9 in the morning and between 5 and 7 at night when people can actually do a lot of work without the phones ringing. We don't schedule internal meetings on Monday and Friday, so there is much more time on those days to get work projects done. When we saw, after four months, that we were meeting our time lines, projects were being finished on time, member service complaints didn't go up, our board of directors voted to extend the four-day flex week.

At the Federal Reserve Bank of Minneapolis, Kathleen Erickson tells us that about 15 percent of the total staff and 30 percent of the women of a forty-person staff are now working part time.

It's been very very positive. The first benefit is elasticity. We have a trained work force that has the capacity to expand or contract de-

pending on the workload. When a project presents a larger amount of work to do than was anticipated, we have in place people that are trained and prepared to do the work. We've gone to our part-time people and said, 'We have a job that needs to be done, are you willing to put in a few extra hours this week?' As long as they could see that it was finite, they were more than willing.

The second benefit from the employer's standpoint is the retention of human capital. Today, with computers and the nature of the work we do, an employee that has been trained costs about $12,000 over the space of twelve to twenty-four months. All the employees currently working part time could have been lost if we hadn't offered a part-time option. If they left, I would have had to start over, reinvest those training dollars, and lost productivity while new workers were being trained.

From the standpoint of productivity, the part-time people are very eager to make the point that they're pulling their share of the load. We do pro-rate all our benefit programs for part-time employees, vacations, and holiday. They have the same percentage of benefits as the percentage of the full-time work year that they work. Without that it would not be successful.

In Maryland, the Montgomery County government started what it calls a "work/life" program in 1993. Marian Brescia told us how it happened:

We were in a severe fiscal crisis, and morale was low. Since raises were being frozen, and there was very little to offer our 7,500 employees, we came up with a series of alternate work schedules. The first is a compressed work schedule, where people work nine-hour days for nine days, and they're off the tenth day—which can be either a Monday or Friday once every two weeks. About 1,200 employees currently participate with an equal number of men and women represented. Other programs include telecommuting—which allows employees to work from home one or two days a week. We also have job sharing, where two employees working part-time share one job. We also offer flexible work hours, which allow em-

ployees to choose their daily work schedule, as long as they work four hours between the core hours of 9:00am to 2:00pm.

Through our "work/life" program, Montgomery County managed not only to retain its valued workers but also to increase team work—an unexpected result. That's because employees work harder to make sure their work is covered, and they're learning much more because we're all sharing our knowledge. In addition, employees participating in all of these alternate work schedules are traveling half-a-million miles less a year. It is helping us to comply with the Clean Air Act.

The program is a two-way street, helping both the employers and the employees. Employees say it helps to reduce stress and worry, balance their work and life, and gives them more time for families, child and elder care, and for leisure time. Many say we have given them the gift of time, something you can't buy. As an employer, Montgomery County has benefitted from greater loyalty and dedication from its employees, and an increased skill level from pitching in to help each other on the job.

INTERNATIONAL PERSPECTIVES

But it's not that simple. Suzanne Smith, who flies in from San Francisco, has been working for twenty-two years on "flexibility." She is the co-director of New Ways to Work, a national non-profit encouraging the creation of equitable work time options as a means of addressing employment related social and economic needs.

It is developing flexible staffing policies to help contingent workers, the unprotected part-time workers, temporaries, low-paid contract workers, and the unemployed. Through the years employees have strived to figure out how to balance work and caring. Now companies have figured out they have to have flexibility. Where has this kind of demanding company push along with the personal push gotten us? And where should it take us?

Here is an example of work sharing as an alternative to lay offs with specific policy implications. All or part of a workforce tem-porarily reduces hours and salaries but also receives short-time un-employment compensation. Let me explain. In the United States, seventeen states now have laws that allow for short-term unem-ployment compensation. If a company is going to be laying off em-ployees it can keep its team together. If it needs to cut 20 percent, in-stead of firing those employees, it can reduce each employee's time by 20 percent and the employee can draw 20 percent of their unem-ployment compensation while working less. The company does not have a great drain in terms of pink slips and will have the team later on when it needs one. Employees have jobs. Motorola uses this formula.

Despite economic problems, Europe still has a better social net-work for people than we've ever thought of having. The wage for fam-ilies is higher. There's less poverty. Volkswagen added an extra shift in order to create more jobs and cut back the amount of time that the people who were employed on the regular shifts were working. Europe does a lot of work sharing. Demand for the four-day work-week has been developing both in Europe and in Canada.

But Joyce Miller, former union officer and president of the Coali-tion of Labor Union Women, now with the Labor Department, is uneasy:

No one ought to look at part-time work as a panacea. There are women out there who are sole supporters of their families, and they need a full-time job. Part-time work is not a wonderful alternative for those people who need full-time jobs. Second, it's the white males who are taking early retirement or leaving because they're the ones who have been in the work force the longest and they have pen-sions and can afford to leave.

Third, talk about benefits for involuntary contingent and part-time workers. That's important. Part-time work and work sharing are fine for those people who can afford it, but you don't share going to a grocery and buying a loaf of bread. You need money in order to buy that loaf of bread.

A lot of the older workers talk about part-time work if they're union members, and they get a pension, or they get Social Security. For them, to get out of the house and work ten or fifteen hours a week is wonderful. But don't tell that to the single mother who is raising two little children and has to spend her life in a minimum wage job.

In many cases when people talk about part-time work and job sharing, they are talking about women. They think in terms of men having full-time jobs and women only having part-time jobs. It's back to the old sexism that women don't really need full-time work because their husbands will provide for them, but this is a different world. We have to recognize the realities of life.

WHEN WORK SHARING DOESN'T WORK

Geoffrey Cowan, director of the Voice of America, comes to the new paradigm seminar because he tried a variation of job sharing instead of downsizing 250 of his 1,400 employees, as part of "reinventing government." Instead of two people sharing one job, each part time, he suggested that several employees reduce their work and pay by one day. They would work a four-day rather than a five-day week on a regular basis but no one would lose their job. His people, mostly women, liked the idea in principle, but not when it came to their own jobs, Geoff said:

We could have saved all those jobs if enough people wanted to participate in job sharing. I proposed that management lead the way. Managers could cut their time and their salaries by 10 percent, one day every two weeks. You can have more time with your family, more time to get other things done. I explored this with other managers, but in the end, I did not publicly offer the idea of managers doing this. One woman in particular thought it would really embarrass some of the managers, including her, because she really couldn't afford to do it.

In one language service, eight people who were going to lose their jobs took the position that their colleagues should engage in work sharing. If everybody in that division worked four days a week, all jobs would have been saved. In the end, two people lost their jobs. Nobody in the service offered to share, including the six people who had previously wanted everybody else to participate. We were also offering to pay the benefits that go with the job.

Heidi Hartmann concludes that this experience says a lot about where we are psychologically and why we have to educate people to think in new paradigms.

FUTURE SCENARIOS

But something is missing from the new paradigm we are groping for, from the either/or, no-win dilemmas we keep coming back to. We have to include more people from industry, from the corporate world itself, because what's surely implied here is a paradigm shift in corporate definition of the bottom line, as well as our personal definition of success.

What are the future economic projections and past historical precedents, the underlying values and assumptions of the paradigm shift we are working toward? I try to add a broader perspective to our discussion. We bring in Jeremy Rifkin, president of the Foundation on Economic Trends and author of *The End of Work*. He sees a new future, one where there will be few jobs left unless the workweek is reduced and value is put on the "third sector" of volunteer community work. Jeremy Rifkin tells us:

In the early part of the century when agriculture mechanized, the manufacturing sector absorbed that surplus from labor. When the manufacturing sector began to mechanize in the late 1950s, the service sector absorbed that surplus labor force. Now all three, agriculture, manufacturing, and service, are moving toward a higher degree of automation. The sector emerging to absorb the surplus labor, the knowledge sector, is a very small, narrow band: the consultants, lawyers, programmers, engineers, and scientists. The real angry vote in November 1994 had nothing to do with the Republican programs or the Democratic programs. *The focus group after the election found out that working Americans' main concern was anxiety over becoming underemployed, unemployed, or being reduced to temporary just-in-time workers. It was that anxiety, that angst, that frustration that was vented at the ballot box in November. Unfortunately, there wasn't a single candidate in the country speaking to that issue.*

With the government less able to be an employer of last resort—in fact with politicians now calling for an end to big government—that opens up only one other arena to deal with the problems that we're going to be facing. That's the third sector: parents' groups, churches, synagogues, women's groups, and civic groups.

Ten percent of all paid employment in this country is now in that third sector. It's the only sector that's really growing (the nonprofit, voluntary sector). There's going to be an increasing burden on this third sector as we drop the social net. We ought to have a tax credit for every hour that people volunteer to a 501-C3 nonprofit organization in this country. We allow people to deduct for charity. We ought to allow individual households to deduct for time given. People who are moonlighting around two jobs or three shifts could have a choice between one extra job or perhaps volunteering in that third sector to help provide the services in their community.

People are not going to find more and more jobs in the marketplace. They're not going to find more and more jobs as public employees. We need to retrain people to work in nonprofit organizations in their community—to build community.

Another option is to shorten the workweek. Corporate America already has. It's called the temp work force, and there are no controls. Twenty-five percent of all American workers are now temp workers, and 35 percent will be by the end of the century. There will be no organized labor movement when we reach 40 percent of the work force as temp workers. You cannot organize a temporary worker in a union.

If we can develop a movement, bringing together organized labor and third sector groups around the idea of moving steadily toward a thirty-hour workweek in the next ten years, we can have a powerful paradigm shift in American labor. A lot of people who are interested in family values want to bring parental supervision back to the family. We should argue for six and six. You're at work for six hours when your children are at school; you come home when they come home.

A goal by the year 2005 should be reducing the workweek gradually and steadily so that there's enough work to go around and enough purchasing power to keep the economy growing. That way we can tie it in with productivity gains so workers will not be punished by their workweek being reduced.

PAST LESSONS

Many of the people, especially the women, in the new paradigm seminar run such organizations. They are clearly aghast at Rifkin's idea that the third sector could take up the slack. Historian Eileen Boris from Howard University revives our spirits by a historical account of the actual campaign that led to the forty-hour workweek and time-and-a-half for overtime in the 1938 Fair Labor Standards Act:

The struggle was led by working people and labor-oriented intellectuals, especially women reformers, and also included business allies like Edward Filene of Filene's department store. The struggle had really two streams. One was collective bargaining, pursued by skilled, mostly white, male workers who relied on union agreements with employers to obtain shorter hours. The second stream was legislation, sometimes known as protective labor laws, first demanded in the 1840s, led by mill girls and women workers who didn't have a vote but could petition the state. The Supreme Court in 1905 refused to extend what was then considered the police power of the state to male workers. If they worked fifteen-hour days, well, that was their right to contract, and government should not interfere.

Legislation for women and children then offered a strategy, an en-

tering wedge to obtain labor standards for all. The famous 1908 Supreme Court case Miller v. Oregon, which upheld maximum hours for women workers, was based on a massive amount of evidence on health, work, and fatigue to argue that long hours undermined their efficiency on the job and in the home. The Supreme Court emphasized biology, women as the weaker sex, and mothers of the race, to justify shorter hours. But women reformers and their male lawyer allies like Felix Frankfurter used similar evidence for both sexes to document the negative impact of a too-long working day.

The Court upheld shorter hours for all workers regardless of sex in Bunting v. Oregon of 1917. Then the progressive tide receded and changes in the political climate in the Court led to the striking down of labor standards that addressed wages.

It wasn't until the New Deal that labor standards again became the major route for unskilled and female workers to gain improved conditions. There was a coalition of Congress of Industrial Organization [CIO] new industrial unions, labor intellectuals, labor lawyers, and a group of reformers around Eleanor Roosevelt.

If we can see these different levels of people in the unions, in state government, in national government, in the voluntary organizations, and in the reform organizations, then we can see perhaps the seeds of what needs to be done as this coalition pushed through shorter hours and other labor standards. The women reformers often worked behind the scenes. They adopted an inside-outside strategy, working in tandem with those inside state agencies.

Could such a coalition be organized today to push for a thirty-two-hour week? Not by and for women alone, of course. The new paradigm would bring women and men together in moving for a breakthrough in their work-time bind. Companies would surely not adapt it as an alternative to downsizing without a struggle if it meant more benefits to pay, as the bottom line is measured in the old paradigm. The union leader from Flint thought it would take an AFL-CIO general strike, nationwide, one, two, three days. Recent studies by the Work and Family Institute in New York show no difference now between women and men in their willingness to trade off some income increase for more time. But the union movement, which today represents only 15 percent of workers in both the public and private sectors, is concentrated on "a living wage," as they must be, and on organizing. The labor movement, the women's movement, do not yet see this work-time bind as the organizing issue it ought to be.

A CURRENT CAMPAIGN

An underground, of sorts, seems to be building up around the idea of reduced work hours, on a Boston-San Francisco axis. It started in 1989 at a conference at Wellesley College on women and work, when the activists and volunteers began talking about the time crunch in their own lives. Barbara Brandt of the Shorter Work-Time Group comes down from Boston to tell us about it:

The newspapers and magazines had begun talking about the harried family, the time crunch simply as an individual problem. Our group was discovering that this is not just an individual problem or a family problem, but a social and economic problem. We put together an article, "Less is More—A Call for Shorter Work Hours," which the Utne Reader *ran in July–August 1991. We got letters from all around the country from men, women, and married couples of all ages, and all backgrounds. We started a newsletter, began to get in touch with others activists around the country. Finally we decided we needed a national coalition of all the different groups and activists who were interested specifically in the work-time issue.*

Our group is now part of a grassroots network of people and organizations in the United States and Canada concerned about shorter work-time. We discovered there are a lot of ways to help people reduce their work hours. For those people still lucky enough to have full-time jobs who are being increasingly overworked, we need to prohibit compulsory overtime or charge employers a penalty by paying extra for the overtime.

For people who are at the bottom of the scale and are forced to work more hours because they can't make it on a forty-hour week, we need to raise the minimum wage. If full-time employees in their workplace are getting vacations, pensions, and health benefits, part-time workers should get pro-rated benefits. Finally we need to reduce the full-time standard from forty hours a week to something like thirty-five or thirty-two or thirty. Many people we talked to also said they want longer periods of time off, such as a longer weekend or sabbaticals.

This is the first concrete policy implication of the new paradigm. It doesn't fit somehow in the current focus of either the women's movement or the labor movement. "The new paradigm implies larger values and new values for community," I say. "The process of building a new coalition for the new paradigm will be as important as the effect."

SOCIAL CAPITAL AND CIVIC VIRTUE

We now read Robert Putnam's study of Italian city states ("The Prosperous Community: Social Capital and Private Life," *The American Prospect,* Spring, 1993). Sandra Myers had been conducting dialogues for the National Endowment for the Humanities on values Americans agree on. She points out what is important about this study:

What Putnam and his colleagues discovered was that party politics or ideologies or affluence made little difference in determining which twenty new regional governments were successful in managing the public's business efficiently and satisfying constituents. Instead, the best prescription for success was strong traditions of civic engagement: voter turnout, newspaper readership, memberships in choral societies, literary circles, and Lion's Clubs. New paradigms are based on new assumptions. Can we assume that cooperation might work better than competition, that civic mobility, public mindedness, and concern for the common good are as important as individual success? We're a pragmatic people. We need to change paradigms if the old one doesn't work anymore. I propose that we consider social capital, civic virtue, and building social networks as guiding principles for the future. We will need the best thinking of the civic voluntary sector to advocate change. We will need visionary public officials to reshape public policy.

But many of the members of the new paradigm seminar, heads of nonprofit voluntary organizations themselves, are very dubious at the prospect of "the third sector" taking over those functions of protecting health, welfare, child care, the environment, and other community services that politicians now propose abolishing or reducing.

Heidi Hartmann protests:

This is the most ridiculous thing I have ever heard. Where are the resources going to come from to run these organizations? Right now funds have come largely from the public sector and secondarily from individual contributions from people's wages. Is this the last cry of failed capitalism that they think the nonprofit sector is going to solve all our social problems? The reason the government subcontracts with all these nonprofit groups to deliver community services is not because they're more efficient, it's because, in effect, they can pay workers less. In effect, they exploit women and minorities who work disproportionately for nonprofits.

I was thinking of a more active kind of community volunteering, the kind that built the women's movement and many of the innovations of American democracy, from the civic groups that played so strong a part in Peoria, Illinois, where I grew up, to the PTA on which I helped innovate better education for my kids during my housewife years in Rockland County, New York. Real volunteer activity such as that that built the women's movement—before it got to be a matter of paid staffs and million-dollar office budgets—has been a basic contributor to the progress of American life. If you're going to spend less time on paid work, why not get a tax credit for volunteer work?

Karen Narasaki of the Asian Pacific American Legal Consortium says: "Let's say that we're all pushing for a shorter workweek. Multinational corporations will just say, 'Fine, we'll move overseas and we'll hire sweatshop workers.'"

Heidi Hartmann suggests:

We could try to focus attention on corporations and what corporations are doing, monitoring them, grading them A,B,C,D,E. It's interesting that the management gurus are pointing now toward the third sector. Perhaps the for-profit and non-profit sectors could find common ground, especially those corporations concerned with the private sector, for improving labor standards.

Barbara Reisman, Child Care Action Campaign, says one of the things standing in the way of better child care is the fact that parents don't want more child care, they want more time with their kids. This is an opportunity to unite mothers at home with mothers who are in the workplace. Surveys show that what most mothers of young children want is to work part time with pro-rated benefits. That's increasingly true of some fathers.

Washington Post columnist Judy Mann is "struck by the possibility of talking about more parental supervision at home—the 6 and 6 idea as a way of really beginning to define family values in an important, meaningful way that does affect families. Also to think about this in terms of health care. When people are living these very stressed existences, they are getting sick at much greater rates. Part of what's going on with breast cancer has to do with the very highly stressed lives that some women are living."

Putting all these ideas together, we take a first step to get visionary public officials, corporate and community leaders, to confront the need to transcend the old ways of thinking about these things. I write, with the group's approval, a letter to President Clinton suggesting hearings by a Presidential Commission on Economic Changes and Family Stress. We offer our services to help carry out such hearings, but the White House seems struck dumb by the explosion of the "angry white male" backlash in the 1994 election. Some months later I get a perfunctory note that my letter has been forwarded to the Domestic Policy Council.

4

WELFARE REFORM, AFFIRMATIVE ACTION, AND BACKLASH

Everyone is now talking about "the angry white male." Newt Gingrich and the Republican newcomers elected in 1994 who are running Congress and, it seems, the government—with their Contract with America to end government—are making the president seem irrelevant. The whole thrust of American politics seems to be getting rid of programs and policies protecting women, children, and families, the environment, our health, workers' safety, clean air and water, pure foods, safe drugs, education and arts, infants and elders, and the taxes that support them, in the interest of unlimited corporate greed. Even Clinton is promising to "end welfare as we know it" and "end big government." The media reports that corporate lobbyists are now openly marking up the bills in congressional committee offices.

And, just as I feared, the backlash against women and minorities is becoming more visible. The "balance the budget" hysteria now reveals specific slashes or elimination of programs affecting children: "Head Start," the nutrition and health programs for pregnant women, mothers, and infants, immunization of kids, and Aid to Families with Dependent Children, which will push millions of children into poverty. Women will be the main victims of the proposed drastic cuts in Medicaid, Medicare, Social Security, and welfare.

GOP Outlines Broad Welfare Reform, Proposal Would Replace Federal Programs with Block Grants to States
(*Washington Post,* January 7, 1995)

Republican congressional leaders are finalizing a welfare reform proposal that would replace hundreds of federal programs with direct cash payments to the states, a wide-ranging change that would allow states to create their own welfare systems with little direction from Washington. . . . Perhaps the most radical change would end the entitlement status of AFDC and several other programs . . .

Will the president and the Democrats stand up to the call to eliminate welfare—end Aid to Families with Dependent Children, give block grants to the states with no entitlements or standards protecting the people who go on welfare? And there is the demand now to get rid of affirmative action, which opened all those jobs to women and minorities. The new paradigm doesn't mean, can't mean, giving up our advance to equality with men, our economic empowerment as women, but we will be pushed back if we don't think beyond our own pay equity and career advances compared with men's.

It strikes me, studying the polling data Celinda Lake had shown us earlier, that those housewives or women with the temporary jobs whose husbands have been or fear being downsized, and now have no choice but to carry the wage-earning burden, may not be inspired to come to the polls no matter how staunch Clinton has been on abortion or appointments of top women.

SCAPEGOATING WELFARE MOTHERS

At this point, I am heartened to be asked for help from a new young group calling itself the Committee of 100—students and their professors of women's studies and social work at universities from California to New York, who want to raise their voice in support of the women on welfare. Many of my own students, especially the older ones raising their children alone, had to go on welfare while they were trying to go to school. The NOW Legal Defense and Education Fund, of which I'm a lifetime director, gave the Committee a desk in their Washington office.

I go with them to see half a dozen senators and representatives. They seem demoralized. Senator Daniel Patrick Moynihan, who had wanted big changes in welfare programs himself, is now violently fighting just to keep in place the guarantees and entitlements that exist—otherwise, according to new government reports, a million and a half more children will be pushed into poverty.

They ask me to speak at a vigil in front of the White House, urging the president to stand firm in defense of the women on welfare, as he is beginning to do now, in the face of the attacks on Medicare, Medicaid, education, and the environment. I look around at the vigil and do not see the heads of the feminists' organizations present. Some have announced their priority is saving the right to abortion, also under new attack by some of the freshmen extremists in Congress.

I have coffee afterward with Frances Kissling, head of Catholics for Choice. Like me, she is cynical about the turf battles of the women's movement and the single-issue concentration on abortion—"still the sexiest issue for direct-mail fundraising"—and the silence on the economic issues. She thinks pressure was put on the other women leaders not to confront the president over welfare. Or was it self-censorship, not to incur the wrath of Gingrich's Congress, already threatening to remove the tax-exempt status of organizations, like AARP, that are resisting attempts to cut Medicare, Medicaid, and Social Security.

About this time, I attend a day-long symposium of leaders of women's organizations, educators, and policymakers on getting more women named as presidents of colleges and nonprofit "third sector" organizations. That day, I must have sounded like Cassandra, warning that while we were staring up at the glass ceiling the whole house was falling down. Because the proposed slashing of Medicare, Medicaid, loans for education, and child care, not only threatens the survival of women, old and young, and children, it would saddle the organizations with burdens they can't possibly carry.

But now that I live within the Washington Beltway, I see with my own eyes how removed women and men "policymakers" and media pundits can be from what is happening in the country at large to people's lives. The women leaders do have a press conference, on behalf of the welfare mothers, but the media ignore it. As for affirmative action, the new paradigm has to go beyond it: alternatives to downsizing that would provide more jobs for everybody, not women versus men, or blacks versus whites.

The new paradigm seminar confronts the realities behind the scapegoating of welfare mothers for the troubles of the American economy. We learn that most people on welfare are not black teenagers who keep having babies to get more welfare checks. They are women, not teenage mothers, who go on welfare because they've lost a job or get left by a husband, and get off of welfare when they get another job, get through school, or other job training. Women on welfare need job training and actual jobs, with child care and health insurance.

WELFARE REFORM ALTERNATIVES

Under the old paradigm, "welfare as we know it must end," President Clinton proclaims. The Contract with America proposes to cut unmarried women off welfare if they have babies, cut all women and their children off welfare after a certain number of months, reduce welfare drastically, or turn the whole thing over to the states with block grants. It seems hopeless to defend "welfare as we know it," even for those of us who share my outrage at the demonization of welfare mothers, making poor women and their kids scapegoats of the culture of greed, and its dirty underbelly of growing middle-class economic frustration. Even a sympathetic feminist columnist, Judy Mann, writes (*Washington Post*, January 11, 1995): "President Clinton got it right when he said hard-working Americans who play by the rules are 'tired of watching their earnings benefit people who don't.'"

Under the new paradigm, welfare reform would aim to lower the poverty rate, especially for children, by providing help for working parents—not in the form of cash, but vouchers for child care and health insurance to make it practical for single mothers to get off welfare. Barbara Bergman, professor of economics at American University, joins Heidi Hartmann in presenting their plan, called "Help for Working Parents" which they presented the day before at a meeting of the American Economics Association. At our seminar, first, Heidi dispels the myth of this feckless no-good teenage mother having baby after baby just to collect the welfare money. From Census Bureau data tracking families for two and a half years, IWPR researchers selected a representative sample of women who received welfare for at least two months during the period and find:

Only 11 percent of the welfare mothers in our sample are teenagers, and 91 percent of them live with their parents or other adults. Our data show that 48 percent of them are working. Some of the women work in the same months as they collect welfare, while others are working in the months when they are not receiving welfare. In other words, during the two years studied, they're moving on and off welfare. Many of the rest are looking for work.

The jobs these women have are low wage—$4.25 an hour—jobs like maid, cashier, nurse's aid, waitress, or child care worker. The women on average are about thirty years old and have four or five years of job experience. If they are able to combine welfare with work and family assistance, they are less likely to be in poverty. If they're trying to survive on welfare alone, they're almost 100 percent in poverty. Figure 4-1 shows the considerable labor force activity of welfare mothers.

The deadbeats that policymakers are worried about are really a very small population. We don't need a mandatory program that forces people into work and wastes resources on monitoring and creating make work in government bureaucracies. We propose respecting poor women, giving them autonomy and choice, but also giving them assistance and encouragement to work. We propose doing something about child poverty and not simply maintaining poor people below poverty as they are now with AFDC.

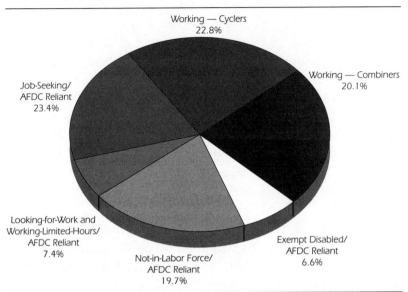

Working — Cyclers
22.8%

Working — Combiners
20.1%

Job-Seeking/
AFDC Reliant
23.4%

Looking-for-Work and
Working-Limited-Hours/
AFDC Reliant
7.4%

Not-in-Labor Force/
AFDC Reliant
19.7%

Exempt Disabled/
AFDC Reliant
6.6%

Source: Institute for Women's Policy Research calculations based on the Survey of Income and Program Participation, 1984–1988, U.S. Bureau of the Census.

Barbara Bergman describes the shortcomings of the present welfare system, which she calls "deservedly unpopular." It discourages work because the jobs welfare recipients can get "don't give them as good a life as they can get on welfare, although the life they get on welfare is a very, very bad one." And the system keeps children in poverty. Bergman continues:

Currently 22 percent of children in the U.S. live in poverty. In western Europe not a single country has as much as 10 percent of its children in poverty.

The Contract with America suggests that we cut off large numbers of children and their parents from welfare. Or bundle everything in a block grant and send it back to the states, taking away their entitlements and food stamps. . . . When the country wakes up from this pipedream about government-free America, we may be able to think about government programs that might do what we need them to do, which is to get children out of poverty and get single mothers into the work force where they can be respected citizens.

Barbara Bergman reports her calculation of what a single mother will have to earn to pay for child care so she can work, pay for health insurance, which she will lose when she goes off welfare, and pay for food, clothes, and modest shelter. It is on the order of $25,000 a year for a mother with two pre-school children. The vast majority of working single mothers can't make enough to pay for these necessities. Bergman continues:

Now, if they are presented with health care and child care, then even a full-time, year-around, minimum wage job, supplemented by food stamps and the earned income tax credit, would suffice to keep a single mother and two children in decency. Because these jobs begin and end frequently, you have to have a fallback, and one possibility would be to make it consist of vouchers with relatively little cash. The child care program envisioned in the "Help for Working Parents Plan" would provide for child care for the poorest 20 percent of parents and subsidize child care on a sliding scale for lower and middle income parents.

This design is like the system they have in France where the state heavily subsidizes child care, pre-school is available free to all, there is universal health insurance and little poverty among children.

Demetra Nightingale, an economist with the Urban Institute, proposes elimination of welfare offices:

The primary public agency in a poor neighborhood should not be a welfare office or an unemployment office but a workers' support office, something like the Agriculture Extension Service. Its main purpose would be helping workers to remain employed, helping them to switch and shift from job to job, preferably up a career ladder. The office would have job clubs people could go to, with available job listings, automated job banks, access to computers, help with educational and job application forms, tax assistance, and civil service testing or other employment opportunities. A separate section would provide "service brokering," letting working parents know where they could go in the community for counseling or help with problems like family crisis or substance abuse or legal issues or child support enforcement.

A third component in the worker support office would coordinate federal community service jobs. It's not politically fashionable today to support public service jobs, but I do. A lot of programs now should be community-based with the individuals, not just the government, having a say in the services that might be needed.

But Gene Steuerle, a colleague from the Urban Institute makes us face hard statistics on how much families now on welfare will lose if they go to minimum wage jobs, or even twice minimum wage jobs. As it is now, they lose AFDC food stamps, Medicaid, and have to start paying Social Security and state taxes. It's even worse if they marry someone on such a job. It turns out that they lose almost 75 percent of what they should have gained by working. It becomes clear that low-income workers, even middle-income workers, pay too much of their income back to the state.

Well, if we are all going to become politically incorrect, I, at least, have to ask him: "Shouldn't we go back to some concept that you tax excess profits more? That you tax very high incomes more or that you tax very high-cost consumption items more? The picture you present is that people on welfare never have an incentive to get off because the low-wage workers are so penalized. But who is going to pay the $86 billion extra for the new child care and health insurance in the "Help for Working Parents Plan"?

Joyce Miller, Labor Department, says, "Let's be honest, a lot of the work they get has to be under the table so they avoid the tax rate." But Diana Pearce of Wider Opportunities for Women says job training and education are the key missing elements—access to nontraditional education as well as college education:

Empowering women is essential because two-thirds of the women who leave welfare for employment return to welfare. Women need to have real job training—education for good jobs—especially if there are going to be time limits. It's the key to empowering women to get themselves out of poverty and into self-sufficiency. And we need a seamless child care system, one where as you move from job training into the work force and as you move up in income, you don't have to move your child to a different program. Minnesota is developing a program like that, including child care and health care, for those who are leaving welfare for employment.

Someone takes issue with Barbara Bergmann's dismissal of block grants as just "more of the same," shifting the burden to the states. "Block grants are much, much worse than more of the same. States want rich people to move in and poor people to move out. Block grants will mean the end of all state assistance to poor people over the next generation. Unless the states are made accountable for lowering infant mortality or something." Someone else says that these "caps" on receiving welfare—two year and out or five years in a lifetime—"what we on the Hill call drop-dead time limits"—are obsolete and impossible to begin with since so many women and men who would like full-time jobs can't get them anymore. They can only find part-time, temporary contingent, or contract jobs.

But how to get a real proposal into the national dialogue—a new alternative to this no-win dilemma, once the scapegoating of the welfare mothers stops? Harriett Woods, former lieutenant governor of Missouri and past head of the National Women's Political Caucus, is worried that we are "going really against the trends." "We have allowed the conservative, nonmajority to pretend their contract is with people," Woods said, "when in fact they simply want to pass the buck from the federal bureaucrats to the state bureaucrats. We who have been in state government know that's the worst in terms of resources and priorities. Can we frame this to put the resources, responsibility, and choice in the hands of the people who are in the communities?"

We go beyond fury at these lethal proposals for "welfare reform" and the defensiveness against the scapegoating of the welfare mothers. The "Help for Working Families" proposal presented earlier by Hartmann and Bergmann offers a real alternative that helps women get above the poverty line and achieve the respectable position of self-supporting adult. But the media does not cover this proposal, coming from these most distinguished women economists.

ATTACKS ON AFFIRMATIVE ACTION

On February 13, 1995, the cover of *U.S. News & World Report* had this question emblazoned in bold type: *Does Affirmative Action Mean No White Men Need Apply?* The article discussed the ongoing debate in America over whether women and men "still deserve favored treatment":

Affirmative action is a time bomb primed to detonate in the middle of the American marketplace. Federal courts are pondering cases that challenge racial preferences in laying off teachers, awarding contracts, and admitting students. . . . On Capitol Hill, the new Republican majority is taking aim at the Clinton administration's civil rights record. On the campaign trail, several Republican presidential hopefuls are already running against affirmative action. And in California, organizers are trying to put an initiative on next year's ballot box banning state-sanctioned "preferential treatment" based on race or gender. A recent Wall Street Journal/NBC News *survey found that two out of three Americans, including half of those who voted for President Clinton in 1992, oppose affirmative action."*

Our search for a new paradigm of community is blocked in the spring of 1995 by the all-out attack on affirmative action. Legislation to abolish federal affirmative action is before Congress, and court decisions are already affecting college admissions and municipal controls. Media coverage plays on fears mined by the actual economic insecurities of downsized white men and more and more women in unprotected contingency jobs. Affirmative action is "the ultimate wedge issue," Republican pollsters exult, and Democratic political gurus increasingly concur.

Yet women and minorities continue to face a "glass ceiling." On March 16, 1995, the *New York Times* reported:

Despite three decades of affirmative action, "glass ceilings" and "concrete walls" still block women and minority groups from the top management ranks of American industry, a Federal commission said today in the government's first comprehensive study of barriers to promotion.

White men, while constituting about 43 percent of the work force, hold about 95 of 100 senior management positions defined as vice president and above, the report said.

Politicians discuss affirmative action almost exclusively in terms of race. I know firsthand that affirmative action has had an enormous effect on opening job doors for women. The National Organization for Women was literally catalyzed into being in 1966 to demand enforcement of the law against sex discrimination in employment. Title VII of the 1964 Civil Rights Act was, at first, taken as a joke.

Until, we got Title VII enforced, employers could and did say, "I won't consider a woman for the job." Women in the telephone company were not allowed to apply for a job beyond operator. When the women's class action suit with its millions of dollars of reparations was won against the telephone company, steps were taken to integrate women, and similarly minorities, into skilled trades and managerial jobs. A few lawsuits like that set the pattern that other companies adopted without lawsuits: affirmative action.

In 1967, I had a hand in getting from President Johnson Executive Order 11246, specifying that companies or institutions with government contracts must end sex discrimination and provide equal employment opportunity to women as well as members of minority groups. They must take concrete steps to end race or sex discrimination, but numerical "quotas" were never required.

IN DEFENSE OF AFFIRMATIVE ACTION

Barbara Bergman, economics professor at American University, completing a book *In Defense of Affirmative Action,* tells the new paradigm seminar she is being plagued by reporters asking how much affirmative action has done and do we still need it. She says:

Those who say affirmative action hasn't done very much imply that we might as well get rid of it, but the truth is we need not less of it but more of it. Enforcement has been very lax. Women have made progress in some companies but not in others.

Banks, for example, have many women classed as managers. At Wells Fargo, two-thirds of the managers are women. Though it has a lot of women customers, the food industry does not have women managers. At Hormel, for instance, only 4 percent of management jobs are held by women. There are many companies where African Americans are almost absent from managerial jobs.

If we abolish affirmative action now, even if we don't go backwards in the places that have made progress, we will be leaving untouched a great many places in the American job market where fair employment is not practiced. White Anglo men working full time still get average weekly pay 49 percent higher on average than the group consisting of white women, Hispanic males and females, and African American males and females. White men still have a huge advantage which is being narrowed only glacially.

Jim Gibson, visiting scholar at the Urban Institute, who had been asked by President Clinton to "review" affirmative action, reminds us that it simply means:

taking "deliberate initiatives" to change institutional practices, to change recruitment patterns, to reach out differently, and to invest in remedial training as part of overcoming past discrimination. The idea that affirmative action introduced "preferential treatment" based on race flies in the face of the fact that preference of white males was standard. What we're trying to do is overcome the insti-

tutional practices that produced that kind of outcome—the prefer-ence for white males.

The discussion of affirmative action now is aggravated by enor-mous, momentous changes going on in this society that cause great insecurity and unease. Whether or not people will have jobs or will have the kind of security in their future that they had anticipated has become a much larger question. We have had a very aggressive income redistribution policy in this country in the last ten to fifteen years—redistribution upward. We have been redistributing a greater proportion of the wealth to a smaller proportion of the population and diminishing, de facto, the people in the middle and below. People feel they're losing ground or losing prospects.

That kind of atmosphere creates the potential for demagoguery. There is a utility to having scapegoats to explain why "I" am suffer-ing or why "I" appear to be hurting. There is also a utility in politics to having scapegoats in times of general unease. The sense of loss can now be pinpointed. It is a way to divert attention away from many of the destructive economic policies developed and imple-mented by the same people who are complaining about affirmative action.

I am glad to hear this distinguished black economist confirm my own sense that the backlash against women and minorities reflected in the attack on affirmative action is designed to take attention away from the increasing polarization of wealth in this country.

CORPORATE EXPERIENCE

But affirmative action does have corporate converts. To big compa-nies, diversity is a business imperative rather than just a government edict. According to the *Washington Post,* March 10, 1995:

Republican members of Congress may be worried that federal affir-mative action requirements are an undue burden on business, but the drumbeat for getting rid of them doesn't seem to be coming from

America's major corporations. "I have never felt a burden from affirmative action because it is a business imperative for us," Mobil Corporation chairman Lucio A. Noto said, adding that it helps the Fairfax-based oil company attract the talent it needs for the future. That's not a maverick view. At many of the nation's large corporations, affirmative action is woven into the fabric of the companies. And the diversity that affirmative action regulations encouraged has become a valuable marketing and recruiting tool, an important edge in fierce global competition . . .

I've been called in as consultant or asked to speak by a number of businesses intent on "managing diversity" in a new way. Xerox, for one, actually encourages caucus groups of women and various minority groups. They have just received the "Glass Ceiling" award for their own affirmative action program, promoting women and minorities. A number of businesses, like Xerox, promote "diversity" for bottom-line reasons. The new paradigm has to include businesses and corporations with a broader vision of community, a more farseeing definition of the bottom line.

Anne Mulcahey, vice president of Xerox, flies down from Canada to talk to us. She tells us that Xerox's stock price actually went up after it won the Glass Ceiling award:

We make diversity part of the business, part of business reviews, succession planning, appraisal feedback, and assessments. For over twenty years now we've worked at it. It's not "today we're going to talk about the business and tomorrow we're going to talk about affirmative action or diversity"—diversity is part of the business process rather than something that sits in the margins. Through a dialogue with caucus groups over the years—we encourage and enhance caucus groups at Xerox that represent women, Hispanics, African Americans, gays—we have made lots of policy and practice changes and changed the way we do business.

When the going was good and Xerox was doing a lot of hiring, we made quick progress. The battle gets tougher because we're not doing much hiring and we've downsized. Our challenge is to see that downsizing is a shared pain. Our biggest problem is maintaining an environment that's conducive to not just diversity but to inspired performance as well.

Companies on the cutting edge of change, the ones moving out of the old static linear model, may be part of the new paradigm. Sidney Harman's company—Harman International—is an unusual American company making over a billion dollars annually in an industry that the United States abandoned to Japan and Korea forty years ago. It is recognized around the world as a maker of the finest professional and consumer high-fidelity music reproducing equipment. Sidney Harman explains how affirmative action is a "piece of a tapestry" for a successful innovative company. He begins with downsizing. Instead of getting rid of workers, he set up a series of off-line production activities, a program called OLE (Off-Line Enterprises) not related to the core business. He tells the new paradigm seminar how this paid off:

We produce loudspeakers. There's a grill cloth in the front and a wood cutout that permits the loudspeaker to operate through the grill cloth. We produce tens of millions of six-inch, eight-inch, and twelve-inch loudspeaker cutouts every year.

For many, many years we paid cartage companies to come and take the damn things away. Now we set up a production line to produce clocks from them, using workers who in other companies would have been laid off. We sell the clocks, give them away, or use them as sales incentives. Now we're growing again, so we've mothballed the production lines for fifteen projects of that sort. We can turn them on in a day if people are relieved of their jobs either through technological change or market circumstance change.

"Change has to be aggressively pursued," he tells us. But he is no wild-eyed dreamer:

Productivity engages us. None of the attitudes that I bring to this public company could survive very long if we were not successful in the traditional way: earnings, earnings per share, balance sheet. But there is incredible room for more efficiency if we will deal with the most fundamental concern people have in their work and that is security. Once people have a genuine conviction about the security of their jobs, they are capable of mind-blowing effectiveness and productivity beyond our wildest imaginings. An earthquake hit our main California plant on a Sunday. Our people drove there through the chaos, worked night and day, and got us operating while neighbor plants were still shut down.

The discussion so far is a piece of a tapestry. We are determined to be an honorable company and you cannot be an honorable company in part. In the hierarchy of business vocabulary, affirmative action is for me the bellwether. It is a strong expression far more consequential than equal opportunity. I dismissed a chief operating officer in our company three years ago for a combination of reasons. One episode that is starkest in my recollection is the moment when we chatted about affirmative action and the inadequacy of what was in process. He was outraged. "We are an open company" he assured me. "Everybody who arrives here of equal skill has an equal opportunity."

In my view that's nonsense. The people we count as minorities are statistically less likely to be of equal skill, and it's a perfect opportunity to discriminate against them. The merit of the phrase affirmative action is that it suggests you got to get out there and make it happen. We go out and find minorities and females.

The session ends that day with Anna Padia from the Coalition of Labor Union Women and the Newspaper Guild (AFL-CIO). She says:

I firmly believe in the development of a new paradigm, especially one that creates a new vision of community. But there are only two words that we need to say about affirmative action: No Retreat. Some people are pushing what we consider "purposeful polarizing politics" to promote old attitudes and stereotypes and push old fears and anxiety buttons. This only deflects from the real issues that we have to deal with: the lack of good paying jobs, downsizing, and *people who want to talk about the angry white male. Well, wait un-til they get a load of the angry working woman who now is begin-ning to understand that this so-called debate about affirmative ac-tion has been very one-sided and is going to be seriously threatening her job, her pay, and her ability to take care of her family.*

When we talk to our white brothers in the union movement, I make this point: "Brothers, many of you have been downsized or re-duced in wages and pay. Because of affirmative action your wives or your sisters or your mothers have been able to get jobs that pay a de-cent wage and have kept the family out of poverty for many, many years." We cannot afford to go back on affirmative action. This is not just a women's issue or Hispanic or Asian issue. This is a family issue.

BACKLASH AND THE MEDIA

You would never guess this discussion could occur from the way af-firmative action is being discussed in the media. The new paradigm seminar holds a joint session with the Women, Men, and Media Pro-ject, which I started eight years ago with Nancy Woodhull, now di-rector of the Freedom Forum's Center for Media Studies in New York. We consider several questions: Are the media colluding in a new backlash against women? Are they dealing with the economic dynamics behind the so-called "angry white male" reaction? Is the picture more complex perhaps than the previous focus of feminists might indicate? Can this backlash, or even its solution, be seen in terms of women alone, women versus men? And yet, are women be-ing left out of the picture as it's being painted by the media?

I ask the roundtable of journalists who have joined us how often the media report the proportion of the budget spent on welfare. It's presented as if welfare is a big cause of the economic misery of the working and the middle class today. Jim Warren of the *Chicago Tri-bune* jokes: "Yeah, somebody in our office joked that 90 percent of the reporters cover 5 percent of the budget."

We talk about the special hostility that Hillary Clinton draws. The negative coverage perhaps reflects a backlash against women with power they didn't have before, except in the home. The women journalists present don't really want to talk about backlash against women in general. It's as if they want to distance themselves from Hillary Clinton. There have been some bitchy stories about her by women journalists. I remind them that when I wrote *The Feminine Mystique* in the late 1950s, all the heroines were sweet, happy little housewives, and when the "career woman" appeared at all, she was a monster. Now, in the mid-1990s, in movies like *Disclosure* and *The Last Seduction*, the career woman is vicious, ruthless, ambitious, and uses sex to reduce men to wimps. There seem to be increasing numbers of custody suits where the child is taken away from the mother, who has a serious job or is doing graduate work, and given to the father who has a new wife or his old mother who is happy to stay home and take care of the kid full time.

Heidi Hartmann, our laid back genius economist, tells us she was on National Empowerment Television, a 24-hour conservative cable network, recently. The callers, she said:

from the sound of their voices were white men, and they all believed that the reason real wages for white men have fallen was affirmative action and they believe affirmative action means putting forward incompetent women and minorities. None of them said, "It's because corporate America is waging an aggressive strategy to pursue profits at any cost, keeping our wages down, and keeping more profits for themselves." It's also to their advantage to try to get the working middle to scapegoat the bottom which is what appears to be happening.

But what the 1994 study from the Women, Men, and Media Project shows us is that women experts are seldom interviewed in the media about welfare, affirmative action, or the economy. It's as if women are an invisible part of the economic backlash. Josette Shiner, managing editor of the *Washington Times*, insists that all the focus on domestic policy issues is "a new phenomenon," triggered by the end of the cold war. As a result, the media are going to have to cover women's concerns in a new way now, as part of the political and economic story, and perhaps changing the terms of the story:

Our paper and most papers in America have had well-trained, well-paid Pentagon reporters but never an expert on welfare and a lot of the social issues that are of real concern to American women. You're seeing for the first time a real spotlight put on these issues, and it's not just the economy. We're seeing the beginning of a major social debate over how our families are organized, how welfare is organized, how we raise our children, the results of the social revolution of the past thirty years, and how we're feeling about it as a country. What newspapers really need to do is put some of their best reporters on these stories and off the defense beats.

Some of the women who've been fighting the gender battle for too many years feel that nothing has changed. Look at the way they treated Eleanor Roosevelt. They see a "culture of inequality." In schools, for example, research shows that as girls start to speak out more, as they speak up 30 percent of the time, boys say they're talking 50 percent of the time and say they're taking over. A male journalist, Warren of the *Chicago Tribune,* notes there was a distinction between white homemakers and career women in the November 1994 election; "the white homemakers sounded like the people calling in to Rush Limbaugh, just pissed off about affirmative action, about everything."

Again, I wonder, is the feminist focus on gender issues adequate to today's problems? The current economic and political reality is being muddied by this idea that there's an eternal gender war, which explains everything and which we can never overcome.

In 1992, a lot of women were elected, a lot more women came out to vote, a lot of men voted for women, and, of course, by a significant majority of women over men, Bill Clinton was elected president with Hillary Rodham Clinton as his wife despite the Republicans' attack on career women and the Dan Quayle–Murphy Brown thing. "The economy, stupid" seemed to affect women's vote.

In 1994, something else happened. There was a play to the white male backlash, overt with the Republicans, acquiescent with the Democrats. ("Off message," they told the serious political women who took "talking points" for women voters to the Democratic campaign leaders.) But at this point, in my opinion, a narrow gender focus—those terrible men will never look at women any differently—is not the issue.

The larger economic dynamics behind the backlash are being ignored by the mainstream media and by the feminist media as well. Is there a scapegoating of women, minorities, and senior citizens to take attention away from the increasing proportion of the wealth of the country now going into the hands of the upper 20 percent, 10 percent, 2 percent, .5 percent of the people? I read the business pages of the newspaper these days. I follow the headlines about downsizing and about the Dow Jones stock market index soaring to new heights. I read about retail stores going out of business, mortgages defaulting, and bankruptcies increasing. But mergers of entertainment and high-tech conglomerates put billions into play.

Do we of the middle class, even those getting a little rich on the stock market and feeling precarious about it, get some relief from our own fears and frustrations by scapegoating welfare mothers, racial minorities, women, older people? Focusing on our own special issues, do we ignore at our peril deeper economic causes and political dangers? Do we lock ourselves into no-win dilemmas by sticking to this narrow single-issue focus, blinding ourselves to the larger power to create alternatives if we held a common vision, a new dream of American possibility, a new paradigm?

5

NEW VISIONS
OF COMMUNITY

Many of my generation in our youth, out of idealism and a passion for justice, out of a sense we had then of our responsibility to make the world better, if we had the luck to escape the limited world of our parents for the larger intellectual life, bought dreams called socialism or communism or liberalism. And we fought a just and necessary war against fascism. After we discovered the unspeakable atrocities of Adolf Hitler's Holocaust and Joseph Stalin's Gulag, we recoiled from larger ideologies and their authoritarian dictates. And reveled in America's freedom, and democracy, and respect for the individual. And put our passion for justice into our own separate battles, those of us who had been denied, for reasons of gender or race, the American dream of self-fulfillment and our individual right to "life, liberty, and the pursuit of happiness."

For those of us who spent our political passion in these movements, the reward was only partly the individual ascent we may have made in career or political or economic power. The real reward was, as Hannah Arendt put it in *On Revolution*, the *participation* in the making of history, the movement itself. The catch-up of equality was banner enough in those heady days, and we became separate communities marching behind it, "the women's community," the "civil rights community," the "gay-lesbian community"—identity politics.

There now seems to be no common American dream stretching into the future—with communism, socialism, the old left and new left, dead, even liberalism apologizing for itself. There is disillusionment with all ideology. How did the women's movement, which thought it was speaking for half of the American people, become a "special separate interest," like a corporation? Can America's future be seen in terms of warring separate tribes, like Bosnia, Croatia, and Serbia?

The new paradigm seminar starts, at least, to talk about new visions of community. The terrible bombing of the Oklahoma government center—lives sacrificed in the name of "enemy government"—gives a sense of urgency to our search. To that seminar in May of 1995, I bring in corporate executives who think beyond the short-term bottom line as well as professors Amitai Etzioni and Benjamin Barber, who have been preaching the need for a larger community or communitarian vision.

WHERE IS OUR CIVIC SPACE?

Benjamin Barber, who holds the Walt Whitman Chair of Political Science at Rutgers University and author of *Jihad vs McWorld*, tells us that the bombing in Oklahoma City put an "exclamation point on every sentence that says America has become polarized and separated into antagonistic interests. We have a cold civil war in America." He makes clear the flaw in defining our separate, special interests—as women, African Americans, Latinos, senior citizens, gays, or handicapped—or letting ourselves be defined in terms of the corporate model. Women and older people are *not* "special interests" in the corporate sense. There is no realizable dream of community if there are just these warring separate "corporate" interests and government. He continues:

Part of that confusion comes from politicians' and political scientists' use of categories to talk about the politics of our country. They play right into the politics of hate and polarization that are on talk radio and in the hate groups across the country. We have been left with two alternatives: big bureaucratic, corporatized, unaccountable, unresponsive federal government represented by some anonymous bureaucracy in Washington on the one hand and on the other hand the private market, special interests, corporations, and the commercial sector. That's our choice, one or the other.

In the political wars here in Washington, the two parties have more or less chosen up along the same lines. Our movements are then required to make the same choice. Those who labor in the union movement, the environmental movement, the civil rights movement, and those who work in the women's movement are all forced to choose. The question is, "Where will you locate yourself?" Do you want to be part of "the private sector," which means your neighbors are the corporations? Or do you want to be part of "the federal sector?" Do you want to work out of Washington where a lot of corporations have their lobbies and their Washington organizations? If they come to Washington and lobby government, then they are seen as simply a part of a set of special interest lobbies that are trying to influence politicians. Where, then, is our space?

Fifty-five percent of Americans now live in suburbs where the primary public space is commercial space made up of malls. There is no other space. There are hardly any churches in our community. There is not a town hall. The schools aren't used any longer as public institutions. There are no town centers or public squares. There are no places where Americans can meet in an ordinary way. There is commercial space; it is understood as private space; and then there is political space, the municipal offices where "the authorities" reside. We don't have—physically, geographically, or conceptually—nongovernmental public spaces where Americans can associate freely with one another in the pursuit of common values.

We desperately need both a geography of political space but perhaps even more importantly a conceptual vocabulary of political *space and of civil society that will permit us to see our activities as common, that will help us to talk to one another about common solutions rather than seeing one another as part of the problem.*

We need to come to an understanding of what it means to be a citizenry, to demand a space for ourselves that is neither in Washington, D.C., nor in the mall, and to find the vocabulary for ourselves that isn't the vocabulary of consumers and private interest, but isn't the monopolistic discourse of government and its clientele either. When we do that, we will rediscover the language of citizenship. Government won't be the enemy, not even the federal government. It will be what it is, just one more extension of how we work and cooperate together in a pluralistic world to find common solutions.

Listening to Barber, I think of "bowling alone" instead of "bowling leagues" as more than a metaphor for women and for men. The decline in membership of PTAs and League of Women Voters he and Putnam talk about is blamed on women working. Women used to do most of that volunteer civic work though men chaired the boards. How did feminism get translated into abdication of voluntary civic community service when the women's movement used to be the most passionate voluntary service to a larger community most of us ever did?

Amitai Etzioni, professor at George Washington University and president of the American Sociological Association, warns that somewhere in this progression "many of the progressive forces got into a terrible fight. We have to find a new way for those of us who consider ourselves progressive to talk with each other as we face the backlash." For instance, he sees the California initiative to end affirmative action as aimed "to divide Democrats against Democrats, minorities and women against each other, and deeply embarrass any progressive candidates by giving them a false choice to fuel racism and sexism." Etzioni continues:

I owe to an African American friend of mine a slogan, "We came in different ships, but we now ride in the same boat." We should not forget different traditions, different needs, different backgrounds, but

we should also remember that we have some shared progressive pur-
poses and community purposes. We have layered and complicated
loyalties. We are challenged by a tidal wave which we need jointly
to face. Working out the language and the vocabulary for allowing
us to do that is an important part of the new paradigm.

AMERICAN IDENTITY

As the chairman of the National Endowment for the Humanities,
Sheldon Hackney was given the mandate to find the values that unite
Americans by initiating "A National Conversation on American Pluralism and Identity." Hackney tells us of a poll done by the Lou Har-
ris organization periodically since 1966. It asks a national sample
of Americans how much confidence they have in a long list of
American institutions—the military, the church, higher education,
schools, the government, the press, Congress, and doctors. The press
and Congress rank very low, the military highest. But the levels of
confidence Americans feel in all these spheres rise and fall together,
and an index based on all these measures since 1966 shows "we are
at the lowest level of public confidence in the institutions of American life. This is a measure of fundamental alienation or lack of confidence in American society."

He says that none of the existing models used to explain an American identity work anymore: assimilation into the beliefs, behaviors,
and attitudes of the dominant Anglo culture; the melting pot of one
national identity, one national culture; or pluralism—a federation of
separate cultures that really don't interact and intermingle very
much. Not sure they explained the past either, Sheldon Hackney
continues:

It is time to try to figure out if there is another model. My own as-
sumption is that we would make greater efforts to ameliorate many
if not most of the problems that we can all list (children having chil-
dren, violence, disparity of wealth, decaying infrastructure) if we
identified with the people who are being most affected by those

problems. We don't know them. We have withdrawn from each other. We have withdrawn from the public square. We sit in our suburbs or our aged cities or in front of our television sets or computer terminals and we don't come into contact with people enough to identify with them.

First, any new model for an American identity must take account of historical reality. There has been a great deal of assimilation that has gone on in America and at the same time a great deal of persistence of pre-American cultural identities. Second, the typical American wants to have an identity that links him or her to all other Americans. They want some commonality, but they also want to retain their connection to their own racial or ethnic or national identity.

Third, Americans believe in mobility. Americans believe in social mobility and in geographic mobility. This is a kind of freedom or liberty for most Americans. That is also true about one's identity. We have to provide for people to travel from one identity to another identity, not only over generations but also in a single generation, the same person at different times.

The American identity must start with commitment to the idea of democracy, which is what holds us together. We're not a race. We are held together by a political idea. That was the original notion of America and it still is. In that idea of democracy is the twin commitments to liberty and equality.

NEW CORPORATE COMMUNITIES

I invite people from the corporate sector to respond. I'm in dead earnest about this new paradigm, and I'm not interested in an abstract, fuzzy idea. The glory of the women's movement is that it came from the concrete lives of women and applied American ideals of democracy to that life. Where the women's movement has been absolutely on target, it has continued to feed into real life and open a larger life to women.

I ask people from the corporate sector who see the corporate task including values beyond the culture of greed. They maybe are beginning to have a larger vision of American community. It's very important to get their sense of the possibilities, I tell the group, because we all know the business of America is business and that's what controls a lot of things and to ignore that is not to deal with reality. Diane McGarry is the president/CEO of Xerox Canada, which prides itself on diversity and affirmative action and its philosophy of participative total quality management. Xerox actually pays for its workers to take sabbaticals to do community service, she tells us:

Our corporate paradigm shifted a long time ago. The problem for some in corporate America is that we have a duty to our workers to be profitable, to be competitive, and to be productive. All the restructuring, downsizing, and information technology changes, however, have forced us to rethink what's happening and have caused confused, bewildered, cynical workers. Most of them were blindly loyal. Now we're wondering how to win back their loyalty.

We've moved our workers to a virtual workspace. Many of them work from homes. They work from their cars. They work from their customers' offices. We network them as required for their responsibilities. We've also moved people and processes out of head offices to decentralized locations, and we've moved the responsibility and the accountability to these people.

In 1971 we adopted a Social Service Leave Program. This policy will pay a worker full time, including all the benefits for up to nine months, while the worker goes out and does some community service, whether that's counseling a drug addict or helping to rebuild a shelter for battered women. The individual worker brings the proposal to a committee of other workers, not managers, and that committee selects the twenty or so people per year who get to do this. They're guaranteed a job when they come back.

Work from home, employee assistance programs, training people how to use their new-found accountability, these are all things that don't just happen. You have to build them into a program or a policy.

Alison May is the CEO of Patagonia, a company in the West that is profitable but also has a vision that profits mesh in some way with larger community values and the environment. Patagonia manufactures clothing for high-risk and general outdoor activities: about $150 million in sales, about 600 full-time employees, a mail order catalog, its own retail stores and distributors. She tells us:

Patagonia was set up right at the beginning by people who hated business, and they wanted to try something that would be different. They wanted to see if a company could be a tool for social and environmental change. We operate knowing that we're in the midst of a social and environmental crisis, and we do certain things that are very different. We have a self-imposed tithing program. One percent of our sales or 10 percent of our profits, whichever is higher, goes to small grassroots social and environmental activists groups trying to do something within their own communities. We'll give away about $2 million this year, and that will probably go to about 600 groups.

[We] at Patagonia spent much of the last twenty years fighting everybody. We finally realized that the polarization that comes from confrontation is not going to solve any of the problems. We subtly changed, and started to form partnerships with other organizations. One program is working with other companies and sharing expertise instead of trying to keep things proprietary, especially in the environmental and technological fields. We worked with a company making fleece products and changed the process to make them out of recycled soda bottles. We gave the technology away so that everybody would use it. This creates a different type of organization. If you try to hold on to technology and you patent things, then you become a reactive organization instead of a creative entrepreneurial organization. We're going into partnerships with the enemy actually.

I have started speaking a lot at business schools where things are going to happen. The youth of America see that they have no future. They question the corporate finance concept of net present value that determines virtually every single decision that's made and forces you to rob from the future. They question the concept of growth and how destructive growth is.

EDUCATION AND THE ARTS

Peggy Cooper Cafritz and I have fought together the good fight in terms of women's rights and civil rights and the need for new thinking and a new paradigm. She is the founder of the Duke Ellington School of the Arts, a pioneering educational institution in Washington, D.C. Her reaction to some of this is that we already have lots of public spaces, activities that draw people together, that draw families together, that could be used to further the public discourse. She describes the coming together of blacks and whites at her school:

At Duke Ellington School of the Arts, about 60 percent of our students come from the worst neighborhoods in the city. They would be classified as poor, school lunch, no chance of going to college, etc., etc. The other 40 percent of our students come from middle class and upper middle class homes, a significant portion of them are white. We have not had a racial problem in the school. Not because these kids don't come from wildly different experiences and not that they don't have wildly different possibilities for the future, but there they have a common goal.

IS CHANGE POSSIBLE?

To end with, I ask two friends of mine in the corporate world this simple question. Suppose you have a campaign for a shorter workweek, the abolition of mandatory overtime, pro-rated benefits for part-time or flexible work, and pay for a five-day workweek but give the fifth day to community service. Is this conceivable in the corporate climate of today? Gene Kofke was a vice president of AT&T when the class action suit was won that made AT&T open its doors to women and minorities. He was working out the policies that integrated women and blacks into the AT&T work force. Since the breakup of AT&T, he is a consultant to many companies on participative management. He said "no," not with job downsizing and international competition:

Right now the things you mention would be greeted by a lot of managements with the same enthusiasm that they would reserve for a huge increase in the capital gains tax. It's possible to get change, but slowly and with great difficulty. Now there has to be some redefinition of what it is that will offer value to corporations—the idea that you serve corporate interests when you advance the community interest as well. Because if markets deteriorate, if the level of public discourse is all violence and self-serving, it's not a good environment to do business in.

Barbara Blum, head of the Adams National Bank, was asked the same question and said "yes" in "bottom-line terms":

My business is a bank and a bank holding company. It is women-owned and our board is small, five women and one man. It's half majority and half minority. Of our four top managers, there are three women and two men. We simply chose the people that we thought were the best.

The board has a value system that permeates the entire organization. Banks across the United States have been complaining about the Community Reinvestment Act, which is putting money into loans that traditionally banks haven't made or putting money into neighborhoods that had been red-lined. Fifty-five percent of our loans are in those communities and are to those people and are to public interest organizations. During the recession, although we lost money like a lot of banks did, we were always well capitalized. None of those loans failed. The loans that failed were the loans to developers—the traditional loans. Yet just last week Congress weakened the Community Reinvestment Act because bankers said this means making loans to people who won't pay you back. Well, that isn't true. By having a board with a value system, we have a new paradigm.

The new paradigm debate is shaping up. There's got to be conceptualization and language for a new movement, a merging of movements, not the kind of confrontational movement that we had before. Our discussions are a groping beginning. I remind them the first step in any revolution is consciousness. Joy Simonson, veteran feminist, objects: "I don't like sounding a sour note, but I have to remind us about all the ill effects that are coming from the downsizing, especially the problems of the contingent work force and people who are laid off in the downsizing who don't have benefits and want to get new training. Shrinking the corporate world may make some individual corporations more profitable, but by and large it has not been beneficial for our national community."

The devolution of responsibility that we're seeing, the reinventing government idea, is saying push the responsibility down and out to the people and the people will solve the problems. Except that when you push it down and out to the fragile organizations that citizens are involved in, they can't meet the challenge. Not that they don't want to. It's a terrific burden. You're taking the most stressed people in the world and asking them to solve the nation's problems with practically no resources. When we talk about paradigm shifts, we also have to talk about resource shifts.

Professor Barber reminds us that Clinton was recently asked about liberals and conservatives, about whether that distinction is valid anymore. His answer was no, we need a new language, and our two parties are organized around a set of differences that aren't really very relevant anymore. Professor Barber continues:

We forget that there are real conflicts of interest in America. There are costs, and not everything can be solved painlessly. I have a problem with our corporate friends when they talk about downsizing and forget that downsizing means disemployed Americans in the end. There are things corporations can't do unless they're willing to become less profitable. They're probably not going to do it. To that extent they're going to be part of the problem before they can be part of the solution. The new paradigm can't pretend there are no conflicts, there are no real distinctions of interest. It has to understand the political action works through conflict. It doesn't run around conflict and pretend it's not there.

So we can agree that we are searching for a new paradigm that does not go back on the advances that the women's movement, the black movement, or the gay rights movement, all of these separate movements have made, and that confronts the reality of American economic life today. Social scientists ten years ago said there were no common values. Maybe they were wrong. The response to the Oklahoma City bombing shows there are common values. If a comparable tragedy had happened in New York, there could have been a response showing common values.

We have to begin from our separate movements whether it's the women's movement or civil rights movement or corporate America because there is a felt need. There are conflicting interests. We can't ignore those interests. But we still need a vision beyond that, of our common good.

THE SUMMER AND BEIJING

New York senator Daniel Patrick Moynihan nominates me as a delegate to the White House conference on age. I get very frustrated trying to get the conference participants to call for Medicare or other health insurance for families with children, as we ask them to help us fight against cuts in Social Security, Medicaid, and Medicare. It is right that we protest strongly against cuts for older Americans, for ourselves, but wouldn't it be stronger to see ourselves in alliance with future generations? There is a threat of intergenerational warfare in the increasing media reports of baby boomers or twenty-something Generation X-ers grumbling about Social Security being taken out of their wages when the likelihood of their ever collecting Social Security themselves is less than a space alien landing from another planet!

The violence of the politics of hate, through much of 1995, seems a national epidemic out of control. The big women's organizations organize new direct-mail campaigns for more money to defend abortion clinics under attack. Charges of sexual harassment rock the NAACP. John Sweeney announces he is running for president of the

AFL-CIO on a platform of new militancy for labor, but the Caterpillar strike in Peoria, my hometown, is lost, and businesses owned by my Republican high school classmates are near bankruptcy.

The only passion, the only unity behind a common dream seems to be coming from the "revolutionary" Republicans—the 104th Congress freshmen led by Newt Gingrich and the religious right preachers and talk show hosts. Their "revolution" is not a new paradigm, but a devolution to some America that never was, for a democracy no longer committed to the protection and advancement of all its citizens.

The enormity of women's new power, as the whole world can see it at the United Nations Fourth World Conference on Women at Beijing in September 1995, is awesome, as my grandsons would say. I remember the First U.N. Conference on Women in Mexico City twenty years ago, where most of the official delegates were men, or their wives and secretaries who gave up their seats to the men when votes came up. The women from the nongovernmental organizations had to march to get a space big enough to meet in, and we shared our concerns as women across national boundaries.

The real message of the Beijing meeting is the meeting itself, the expression of women's new political power with 40,000 women, mainly from nongovernmental organizations and movements the world over. There is an attempt to trivialize or marginalize that power by penning these women up in the isolated suburb of Hairou. Obviously threatening to authoritarian power in China, these militant women are not allowed to get close to the Chinese people. They get their business done anyhow.

When they are told they can only demonstrate in a child's playground, CNN and Hillary Clinton carry their protest to the world with Hillary Clinton stating, "Women's rights are human rights and human rights are women's rights." I lead a workshop at Beijing urging that we now move "From Backlash to New Vision." The document that comes out of Beijing asserts, as a basic human right the world over, a woman's right to control her own sexuality and reproductive process. It makes violence against women, abuse in the home and the street, and genital mutilation of little girls a crime. It suggests that the GNP of all nations include the work now done by women in the home and in the community. This work, paid too little still, or unpaid, is to be valued now as part of that GNP.

All over the world, with women now facing eighty-year life spans and in increasing control of their own reproductive systems, sexual politics will no longer be the main issues defining them. With enormous skill, the women delegates at Beijing resist attempts by the Muslim nations and by the Vatican to vitiate that new assertion of women's right to control their sexuality and childbirth. There is a last-ditch battle to keep women from moving openly on the street in Muslim countries and one to keep women fighting over abortion in the United States, though courts, Congress, and national opinion polls have long since established women's right to choose. Is abortion really the most important problem women face in the United States today? How shall we use this new power, keep it from being marginalized and trivialized, as they try to do in Beijing?

Some of my sisters are preoccupied with the backlash now, the attacks on Hillary Clinton, the Whitewater hearings, the subpoenas. A reporter from a major national newspaper tries for fifteen minutes to get me to say something bad about Hillary. What I say is that whatever she's been accused of doing seems completely insignificant and irrelevant to the concerns of our government and nation.

Unlike some of my sisters, I think it is fine when Hillary has her picture in *Vogue* in black velvet. She is, after all, a great mother, a wife without whom her husband wouldn't be where he is today, a wife who stands by her husband, and puts up with his trespasses. There's an interesting new reality, a new kind of equality and balance of power to their relationship. What's important to women, I tell that reporter, "is what the president is doing now to defend Medicare, Medicaid, Head Start, and welfare food programs necessary for poor women and their families. The media should be ashamed of themselves for making Hillary a red herring."

6

THE NEW PARADIGM AND FAMILY VALUES

Are we allowing ourselves to be divided against each other by leaders intent on channeling our frustrations for their own power? The Million Man March, with its undertone of antisemitism and its exclusion of women, is seen as a wonderful expression of black men's new empowerment. For what? I'm uneasy at the polarization of blacks and white women over the "not guilty" verdict of O. J. Simpson for the murder of his wife and her friend. The extremists of the religious right—and some of the feminists' own extremist rhetoric—have tried to polarize women: feminism and abortion as opposed to "family values."

There's been a false polarization between feminism and families. In recent years we have seen "family values" or "the family" used in attacks on feminism and on the women's movement to equality, as if the two things are opposite. The term "family values" is then used as a flag. At the Beijing conference on women, for example, a woman's control of her own reproduction, or sex education for children, or women working, are viewed as a threat to family values.

Yet when I say there has to be a new vision of family and community some of my feminist friends are resistant to the discussion of family. They say we have been defined too long in terms of family, and we have to think of ourselves first, of women first. Yet if you analyze the values that are implicit and explicit in the Beijing conference, you will see that those values are the values of people first, a concern for the well-being and the welfare of women, men, and children, of old and young.

As a mother of three and grandmother of six, I'm one feminist who is a passionate believer in the value and the importance of families. To turn our back on the values that have rightly been associated with women or what some might call family values would be something I as a feminist would strongly object to and so would many others. We have to get down to brass tacks about family values in terms of realities. We need to talk about what we all mean by family values and how these values can be dealt with, strengthened, and affirmed in terms of today's realities.

In the fall of 1995 I decide to conduct the second new paradigm seminar on reframing family values and to engage in real dialogue with some of the conservatives who now control Congress, but do not necessarily all agree with their own extremists. I am not sure that the new paradigm fits into the left-right polarization anyhow.

Chester Finn, now at the conservative Hudson Institute, former assistant secretary of education in the Reagan administration, Josette Shiner of the *Washington Times*, Dorothy Gilliam of the *Washington Post*, my old futurist friends Alvin and Heidi Toffler, and others agree to join us in the new paradigm seminar to "reframe family values" in the light of new realities. We deal with family values not just in terms of rhetoric but the changing economic and political realities American families face today.

DEFINING FAMILY VALUES

Chester Finn, John Leo of *U.S. News & World Report* and former editor of *Commonweal*, and others see "family values" in terms of a morality now threatened by great increases in unmarried mothers, teenage pregnancy, abortion, and divorce. Finn suggests that we try to alter current realities to pay greater deference to family values and offers the following proposition: "Children need families, and the kind of families that children need are optimally two-parent families that raise them, a mother and a father. No social safety nets and no alternate familial arrangements quite substitute in terms of the well-being of children for some version of a mother and some version of a father, living under the same roof, preferably married."

He goes on to discuss the field of education where he has spent most of his time: "One of the most striking facts is that a child, a young American at the age of eighteen who has had perfect attendance at school from kindergarten through high school, has spent 9 percent of his or her hours on earth in school and 91 percent not in school. It has struck me hard that 9 percent of a young person's life may be sufficient to get them a certain amount of reading, writing, and arithmetic and perhaps even some chemistry and history and geography, but 9 percent is not going to do the job of raising that child if the other 91 percent is in decay or indeed if the other 91 percent is not cooperating. So, one of the ways of thinking about family values is as the organizing framework for the 91 percent of the child's life that the schools have little or nothing to do with."

Dorothy Gilliam, out of her African American experience, sees the family as "the most basic institution of any people, its center and the source of its civilization." She says:

We know that it is in the context of the family that people develop their self-concepts, their values, and their worth and work in relation to others in the world. But the family is not an independent unit in society. It's dependent on other institutions in the larger society for its definition, survival, and effectiveness. Now what is a definition of a value? A value is a choice that a person makes on a consistent basis after having been given a variety of things to choose from. For African-American families, a "shortage of options" defines some of the problems we're facing today.

But the reality, Gilliam says, faced by young parents under the age of thirty today is the inability to make a wage that sustains a family:

"Census figures show their earning power has declined by 30 percent and among African Americans by 50 percent. When the family crumbles because fathers can't get work or when there's not enough income to sustain them, that undermines family values. I'm a pretty practical person and clearly to me the answer of how you support and value families in that context is 'jobs.'"

Isabel Sawhill, an economist at the Urban Institute and formerly in the Clinton administration, documents with graphs and tables two major economic problems: stagnating incomes and the growing inequality of incomes (Figures 6-1 and 6-2). She notes that those with

FIGURE 6-1   GROWTH OF REAL GDP PER PERSON

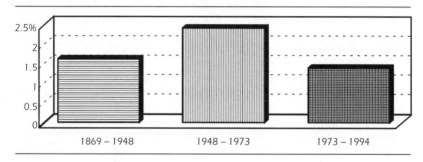

Source: Herbert Stein and Murray Foss, *The New Illustrated Guide to the American Economy* (Washington, D.C.: American Enterprise Institute, 1995), 12–13.

FIGURE 6-2   RATIO OF MEAN INCOME OF THE HIGHEST FIFTH TO INCOME AT THE LOWEST FIFTH

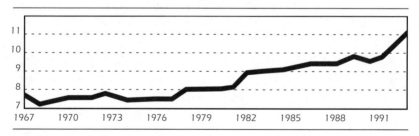

Source: U.S. Bureau of Census, Series P60-184, unpublished data, May 8, 1995, table F-1a. Urban Institute

FIGURE 6-3 ENTRY-LEVEL WAGES, HIGH-SCHOOL EDUCATED MALE, 1973 AND 1993

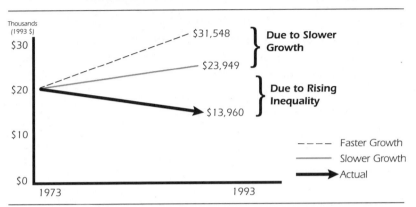

Source: Calculations based on data from Laurence Mishel and Jared Bernstein, *The State of Working America: 1994–1995* (New York: M.E. Sharpe, 1995), 147.

a college education or more have been the ones to benefit from recent economic growth and those with less education have lost. A young man with a high school degree is earning slightly under $14,000 a year compared with the $20,000 he would have earned in 1973 (Figure 6-3).

We all agree that parents have a moral obligation to take care of their own children, that *fathers* are important to the raising of children, and, as *Washington Post* columnist E. J. Dionne, Jr., puts it, "out of the same set of values, there is an obligation to support poor children in our society." We agree on the dilemma parents face today, caught between "defending their children's standard of living by working more or spending more time with their kids." It's worse, though, for the unemployed.

Dionne summarizes two alternative formulations of the moral crisis in the country:

One formulation was Bill Bennett's. When he gave a speech to the Christian coalition, he spoke very forcefully that the crisis in our society was not economic, that it involved crime, family breakdown, illegitimacy, and, as he put it at the time, "just plain trashy behavior." On the other side you have a sense that the moral breakdown involves the pressure on traditional institutions such as the family created by economic change and economic inequality.

Generally, conservatives want to talk a good deal about a very real moral breakdown that stems from illegitimacy and family breakup. Liberals want to talk about the economic pressures created by problems in the economy. In the long run, at the end of this debate that will go on for many years in our country, we have to accept that you can't talk about moral breakdown without bringing both of these factors together.

Other feminists and I do not dispute the evidence John Leo cites that "the children of a single parent family are at much greater risk on every level than a double-parent family." He also deplores the conventional conservative-liberal "split" on family values and provides his explanation of how it developed:

We have to come to terms with 1960s values and 1990s economic problems. Three or four things happened very faithfully in the 1960s. One is the rise of feminism, which inevitably brought severe criticisms of the family as a rigid patriarchal structure. In part this analysis attacked female sacrifice as a dead-end, soul-killing sacrifice for the children. These criticisms brought into disrepute, again with some justice, the very values on which families are based. Both parents, not just the woman, have to live for the child and put themselves second in many ways.

Along with that came the "me decade" of therapeutic analysis: that Americans had been over-committed to sacrifice, that they had to live for themselves, put aside restrictions on their personal freedom, and seek self-actualization and self-fulfillment. This set the stage for a new view of marriage in which the very same spirit that got you into the marriage often pumped you right through the other end. The divorce epidemic really began, I think, with that ethic. Again some value to it. Some people were locked into bad marriages for a long time, but here we see the germination of the wash-and-wear disposable marriage, the ideal of self-fulfillment.

Finally, the controversial Moynihan report in 1965 said economic factors alone were not enough to explain what was happening to the black family. There was a divergence between unemployment and family structure that had never happened before. The opposition said the report was a racist attack on the black family. This controversy stifled and suppressed debate about family structure, black and white, for a whole generation.

That finally is wearing out now, and you're getting some more honest critiques of the American family. But I suggest to you that the split produced by the Moynihan report is still with us today. The conservatives only want to talk about morals, character, behavior, and family structure, and liberals only want to talk about economics and bias. These are bred in the bone instincts, and only now we're beginning to blur them so we can talk about both. It's insane to talk about family problems without talking about both.

Roger Wilkins, Robinson Professor of History and American Culture at George Mason University, counters:

It really blows my mind when rich white guys like Dan Quayle and Bill Clinton lecture black people about family values. In my family, we are like most black people, culturally conservative. We believe essentially in two parents raising a child or children. In my family we have a twelve-year-old child. We have family values. It helps that we've got tenured jobs, one at Georgetown Law School and one at George Mason University. So our kid is nurtured, fed, dressed, all that stuff.

I went back recently to Mississippi where my great grandfather lived after he had gotten out of slavery and was a sharecropper. I found a cousin, Robert, about my age, drunk at 10 a.m. He had family values once. He had jobs in meatpacking plants in Chicago, and then he got into a steel factory, but it went down. By the time I found him, Robert was not only economically redundant, but functionally worthless in terms of family. When they become disconnected from the family, people of both genders and all colors fall apart, alcohol abuse goes up, spouse abuse goes up, drug abuse goes up, child abuse goes up, divorce goes up, and suicide goes up.

There is still enormous prejudice and discrimination in this country. There are neighborhoods that sociologist William Julius Wilson has found in Chicago in which 65 percent of the people in the neighborhood are not in the labor force. Well, I don't know any responsible black people who are not against babies being born out of wedlock. Jesse Jackson has been making that speech for thirty years and so have I. But if the Fed is going to continue to insist that we have a cushion of unemployed people in this country to keep inflation down, if the black unemployment rate is going to continue to be two, three times the white unemployment rate, if we're going to talk about black people's values and morals and never talk about the fact that black people have suffered double-digit unemployment for the last two decades, then we're never going to make progress.

Finally, you might as well spit into the wind as to tell sixteen-, seventeen-, eighteen-, nineteen-year-old people who are economically redundant to forego sex. Hell, they're human beings. If you're a kid raised in a community in which 65 percent of the adults are disconnected from the labor force and you know, as Wilson and his researchers have found out, that the employers prefer immigrants from Mexico who speak Spanish and no English to black native speakers, if you know all that and Dan Quayle comes around and says to you, hey, you're unemployed, I know you got hormones, but wait till you get a job to have sex, well, you're going to have a clash between biology and economics, and biology is going to win every time.

I say to all these people who preach responsibility to black people, do not come to me with this stuff about personal responsibility until you're prepared to be responsible in a policy-making way.

And here John Leo agrees: "When we speak to personal values, we also have to speak to corporate values. Corporations can't just let go individuals, who at one moment aren't making enough money for them, without considering how skilled they are or how much they have contributed. We can't have that sort of value and then say to the individual, you don't have any personal values. We have to broaden this value question so that society has the right values and individuals have the right values."

My definition of family values would be the values of nurturing children that will ideally come from mother and father but must also come from larger family sources and from the community, I tell them. Family values must be part of the priority agenda of the community.

DEFINING THE FAMILY

But there is also disagreement on the definition of the family. Janet Norwood, former commissioner of the Bureau of Labor Statistics and now at the Urban Institute, is troubled that we seem to speak as though there is *the* family, which is the same all over:

The fact is there are many different kinds of families, and each of them faces a different economic reality. The solutions for each of them may not be the same, and the values we develop for each of them may not be the same. It is a mistake to think that there is a set of family values that will fit every single type of family that exists.

They have, however, all been affected by the long-term trends: the declining marriage rates, the increased divorce rates, the changing racial ethnic makeup of families, the substantial increase in labor force participation of women, especially married women, the increased educational attainment of the labor force in general, as well as the virtual explosion of households headed by women in recent years.

Ruth Nadel, formerly with the U.S. Department of Labor Women's Bureau and now from the Clearinghouse on Women's Issues, suggests that we ought to define families as functional or dysfunctional: "A functional family might very well be a single parent. A dysfunctional family might be a two-parent family. But if you have the support of other people, there can be ways of raising children—whether they are in one- or two-parent families—with a strong community and extended family help. We need to talk about child care and jobs. You cannot live on only the minimum wage in today's society."

We agree that divorce is not good for children. But the reality is that many children today are being raised in single-parent families by women alone, not only because of unwed mothers but more so because of divorce. Judith Bruce of the Population Council tells us that this is happening all over the world. Divorce used to be sought mainly by men because only men could afford to move out. Now women have more ability to get out of impossible marriages that can also damage children. But in the new paradigm, truth-telling feminists, and liberals and conservatives, *agree* that marriage and the family should be strengthened.

So we get down to new business, the changes in morality and public policies that are necessary for more men to take equal responsibility for raising their kids. But I can't help asking: what will happen to all those children, too many of whom are already heading into the poverty of single parenting, if the women are not able to earn a living wage and are thrown out of welfare?

Bill Galston left the White House, where he was Clinton's domestic policy adviser, "not to miss the childhood of my own kid," he told me. He also advances our discussion of reframing family values by warning against "false choices." He said: "It's not a question of economic changes or moral changes. It is both. It's a paradox that as the new economy has accentuated the need for more than one source of income to sustain families, more and more families find themselves without two earners."

But he and Leo and the feminists agree that the surge of women into the paid work force is not the only change reducing "family time." A lot of the time we used to spend with one another or in neighborhoods is now spent watching television. I express my own dismay that only 35 percent of American families sit down around a table and eat at least one meal together every day.

Futurists Alvin and Heidi Toffler define the family broadly. Alvin

Toffler explains that the family hasn't died: "We think people want family, they want companionship, they want love, they want community, they want kids, they want to do well by their kids, etc., etc. But one size doesn't fit all, and just as we have demystified and diversified communication, demystified and diversified production, distribution, the same thing is happening with the family and indeed to the political structure."

Heidi Toffler adds:

Today we have placed the blame on individuals rather than seeing that the individuals are victims of a profound transformation in traditional values or what I prefer to call industrial values. We need to invent new social institutions for the third wave. We need some social glue, some generally accepted value system that allows the tolerance and understanding that not everybody is the same and we're not the same.

BACK TO ECONOMICS

I go to the American Enterprise Institute to hear Jack Kemp, Doug Besharov, and others talk about "Empowering Americans: Ending the Welfare State." They now look to "the third sector" to take over welfare. The men on that panel deny that there is increasing income inequality in America—wrong statistics, they insist.

At a brown-bag lunch at the Urban Institute, Robert Samuelson, business columnist for the *Washington Post*, speaks with irritation about "false problems"—"for instance, the *New York Times* series on downsizing—treating as a problem a temporary adjustment of a phenomenon that always has been and will be with us, rich and poor, and nothing can be done about it anyhow." Op-eds begin to appear in the papers saying middle-class incomes haven't really fallen after all, new jobs are cropping up. "Yeah, I've got two of them," a cynical temp tells me.

I go to see Robert Reich, who has been warning in vain of the need to recognize "the growth of the anxious class," the growing numbers of the middle class whose incomes are falling despite the continuing unprecedented soaring of corporate profits and CEO salaries and bonuses. But Reich tells me he is a lone voice, the rest of the cabinet and Clinton's advisers don't want to hear it. It's good for Clinton that the stock market keeps soaring, no one wants to rock that boat.

With all the hype about "balancing the budget" and "reducing the deficit," not even the Democrats get around to explaining, as conservative economist Herb Stein does to our new paradigm seminar, that the deficit is a way of meeting the costs of running the government. Ours is now quite low, he says, and doesn't need to be "eliminated" by reducing services essential to children or anyone else. He concludes, however, that in the United States we don't have a jobs problem:

We have a larger fraction of the over sixteen population employed than has ever been employed in this country except for one year. What we do have is a certain number of people whose productivity when they are employed is less than what we regard as a reasonable level of living in this country. Their productivity when they are employed is higher than most of the world lives on, but it is not as much as we expect even the very poor people in this country to live on. Their productivity has to be raised and that goes back to programs having to do with training.

Julianne Malveaux, economist and talk show host, disagrees. While the unemployment rate, 5.5 percent, is lower than it's been in a very long time, that rate in 1996 is different from what it would have been in 1976: "The temporary sector is growing a lot more rapidly than the permanent sector. We have workers who are on call. There is a level of economic anxiety that no one on the left or right will deny, and *Business Week* and the *New York Times* are talking about economic anxiety."

Herb Stein, however, disagrees and argues that people may say they feel insecure, but they don't behave that way on several economic indicators. He also doesn't think that doing things to keep the top 1 percent or 5 percent of the population from getting richer will do anything to help the bottom 10 percent. The seminar continues the debate begun in 1994 about welfare and welfare reform, about the effects on children and the number of children having children in out-of-wedlock births.

David M. Anderson, who teaches in the philosophy department and at the graduate school of political management at George Washington University, offers an argument for a national family policy that begins to respond to some of the demographic and economic realities. He argues for a policy that would require that the federal government and corporations provide a year of paid leave to parents with newborns and most of the cost of day care for preschool children. It would help relieve stress for working mothers and for welfare mothers. It would unite wives and husbands and enable husbands to be more involved with their children. In the long run it would benefit employers and it would benefit children. "Such a policy, already in place in many countries, would not legislate any moral concept of the family," he emphasizes. "Families would be free to divide up responsibilities as they choose." He suggests, however, that now is not the ideal time to support such a policy, but perhaps by the next presidential election.

The Republicans at the end of 1995 actually shut down government services, refusing to continue month-to-month or day-to-day financing unless the president agrees to their cuts in Medicare, Medicaid, environment, education, and welfare, but the president holds firm. Even the women who didn't come out and vote in 1994 become angry. The *Wall Street Journal* reports in early 1996 that almost all of Clinton's rise in approval rating and the Republicans' fall is coming from women.

Women, it seems, are concerned not in abstract ways about the budget or deficit, or the rise and fall of the stock market but on how they and their families are managing daily life right now, with those not previously affected by downsizing, "on furlough" from the government, or not able to collect their checks.

It makes me angry to read of record new profits when companies like AT&T announce they are going to lay off 50,000 workers. Even the business page reporters comment on how little of that profit is being distributed in wage increases. But it takes Republican commentator-turned politician Pat Buchanan to point the finger at corporate greed as the true villain of the downsizing, although he doesn't hesitate to inflame the politics of hate with attacks on Jewish wealth (as well as on women, blacks, immigrants, and gays).

7

REFRAMING FAMILY VALUES— CHILDREN FIRST

For the first time my newsclips reveal an article based on our new paradigm seminars. John Leo writes for *U.S. News & World Report*:

If you go to a panel discussion in Washington, D.C., on "Reframing Family Values," do not expect much attention to either family or values. Instead you will be flooded with charts and graphs about heads of household and income distribution. The point of this exercise is to show that behavior and values have nothing to do with the crisis of the American family. Everything is economic. If the awkward term "family values" comes up, it will be discussed gingerly as some sort of mysterious and optional product that some households have while others do not. Then back to the charts.

This was true last week on a panel at the Woodrow Wilson Center. When my turn came, I attempted a few chart-free comments. To bolster the family, we certainly have to come to terms with 1990s economics but also with 1960s values, particularly the core value that self-fulfillment is a trump card over all obligations and expectations. By breaking the taboos against unwed motherhood and ca-

sual divorce, we have created the world's most dangerous environ-
ment for children—a new fatherless America filling up with kids
who are so emotionally damaged by their parents' behavior that
they may have a lot of trouble making commitments and forming
families themselves.

An avalanche of evidence shows that single-parent kids are way
more vulnerable than two-parent kids are to all sorts of damage, in
all races and at all income levels, under all kinds of conditions. The
mountain of evidence is just too high to keep arguing that different
family forms are equally valuable or that the quality of the home is
the important thing, not the number of parents in it.

Clearly, not everybody in our seminar is in complete agreement about the meaning of the term "family values," but there is, I believe, essential agreement that at least we mean a community, a sense of commitment and responsibility for community, a climate for the responsible nurturing of children. But we come back again and again to the growing numbers of single-parent families and the absence of fathers in vastly increasing numbers of families as a major cause of economic and social stress and perhaps a generational cycle of poverty and pathology.

There is certainly not agreement about what this phenomenon means, what moral values are involved, or what economic and social realities are involved, but we want to explore this further. It makes me uneasy that this development is always discussed in terms that demonize the mother, the welfare mother, the single-parent mother, the unmarried mother. We need to deal with the causes and effects of fatherless families and what directions in public and private policies and moral discourse might result in more responsible participation of fathers in the raising of children.

THE FATHER PROBLEM

Jim Levine, director of the Fatherhood Project at the Families and Work Institute in New York and author of *New Expectations: Com-*

munity Strategies for Responsible Fatherhood, provides one definition of the father problem:

*"Perhaps the answer to the frequent question 'What's wrong with
modern youth?' is simply it is fatherless."*
That quote comes from Mary Elizabeth Overholt writing in Par-
ents *magazine in 1932. The "father problem" is not exactly new. It
is different now, but putting fatherhood on the table, or citing father
absence as the cause of every major social problem, is something
that occurs in every period of rapid economic and social transformation in America. It happened in the 1890s when men's work
moved from farm to factory. It happened in the Great Depression. It's
happening now in the 1990s.*

Again there are two definitions of the problem, which leads to two
separate solutions. Some people say marriage is the solution, and we
have to promote marriage because it is one enduring way to keep
men attached to their children. Others offer the economic discussion. According to Levine, the data show that "if we provide more
jobs and better jobs to men, especially low-income men, we'll have a
higher likelihood of increasing the rate of marriage and decreasing
the rate of divorce" because the trend lines are just dramatic. While
he thinks promoting marriage and promoting employment are both
important, he sees that paradigm as too narrow. He offers concrete
examples of how changing expectations about fatherhood within the
institutions that deal with families has a positive effect:

*West Virginia over three years quadrupled the rate of paternity es-
tablishment from about 15 percent to over 60 percent. Now how did
it do that? Was there some radical change in the moral or economic
climate in West Virginia? No. They realized that the main point of
contact with young fragile families and fathers, the first opportunity
to establish paternity, was the hospital. And that the maternity
nurse played a vital role in how that young mother and father be-
haved and whether they decided that they would establish paternity or not.*

What they did at a relatively low cost was develop a training program for all of the birthing hospitals throughout the state that basically changed the nurses and administrators from saying, "Look, this isn't our responsibility," to saying, "This is our responsibility and we can do something about it." A nurse can take an active role in talking to that young dad who's scared to death, looking into the nursery at his baby, because he's sixteen or seventeen years old, doesn't have a job, doesn't know what he's going to do.

The nurse can say, "Look, it's important to that child that you establish legal paternity, and it doesn't mean that you have to get married, but it's important you take this first step." Will that lead to more marriage? It might, I don't know. I'm not suggesting that any of these are the magical solution. What I mean by a new paradigm is that it's a step away from moralizing and a step away from looking at the macro problems to looking at every single institution where we live and work and saying what's my role in this. What could our institution be doing? What are our expectations of fathers and mothers?

David Blankenhorn, president of the Institute for American Values and author of *Fatherless America*, offers an eight-point conceptual framework:

1. *The family is a good thing.*
2. *Family structure matters.*
3. *Every child deserves a father.*
4. *Economics matters and culture matters at least as much.*
5. *Community matters and strong communities depend on stable families.*
6. *Bigger government versus smaller government is not the main issue.*
7. *Marriage is a main pathway to responsible fatherhood and improved child well-being.*
8. *The goal is to reverse the trend of family fragmentation, not simply or only to deal with the consequences of the trend.*

It is this last point that leads to very different policy initiatives. He argues that it is not enough to just accept divorce and figure out how to make it work better: "Challenge the trend. We don't just throw up our hands and say, 'Oh, there's nothing we can do about having the highest divorce rate in the world.' We can't just tinker around with child support and paternity ID provisions. Whatever else we disagree on, left versus right, we can agree about an essential goal to increase the proportion of children growing up in stable communities with their two married parents."

Lenore Weitzman, Robinson Professor of Sociology and Law at George Mason University and author of *The Divorce Revolution*, documents some of the problems: only 42 percent of divorced fathers saw their children in the past year; only 50 percent of children receive the amount of child support that courts are ordering. She concludes, "Divorce tends to dispute fathers' willingness to invest in their children both economically and socially, and as a result it disrupts young people's social and community ties. There is a clear link between nonpayment of child support and child poverty in the United States."

Patricia Fernández Kelly, research scientist at the Johns Hopkins Institute for Policy Studies, reinforces the economic links and challenges not only the definition of family values, but of the family itself:

The reason why children growing up in female-headed households suffer more poverty has in large measure to do with the differential incomes of women and men and with the inability of our policy makers and great thinkers to consider how important it is to invest in women. If you actually do a comparison between children brought up by middle-class and upper-class women alone and poor women living alone, you will see significant differences in the outcomes.

We need not to look at redefining family. I am in favor of children who have biological parents held together in some way and working on their behalf. But we who sit in seminars passing judgment on the irresponsibility of fathers and the inability of mothers to raise their children should be finding ways in which we can get involved in the well-being of children.

The family as we know it—with a man serving as provider of the household, responsible for the well-being of women and children and the mother mainly looking after children—was created under family wage legislation at the turn of the century. Prior to that extended families were much more frequent; related and unrelated adults worked on behalf of children, the size of the family was much larger, and the mobility of children was much greater. The so-called traditional family was a strategy deliberately pursued by employers in order to charge men for the responsibility of supporting women and children. Yet how soon we forget the kinds of problems that particular family brought about, including abuses of power on the part of men, distance rather than closeness as a result of the necessity of father to work outside the home, etc.

Chester Finn returns to the theme of challenging current trends:

The continuing irksome aspect of so much of the discussion in this seminar is our unwillingness to challenge the given, and our tendency here to succumb to what we might call economic determinism and demographic fatalism. To take for granted that things must always be the way they happen to be today, that somehow they are beyond anyone's control, that people didn't do them, they just happened, and that people aren't responsible for them, people are victims of forces beyond their control.

We keep referring in this oddly impersonal way to the "phenomenon" of fatherlessness. Well, it's not a phenomenon. Fatherlessness is invariably the result of one of two actions: somebody impregnating someone and not marrying her and living with the child, or somebody having been a father and breaking up. These are conscious actions, controllable actions, actions that people take that I respectfully suggest are also immoral actions when children are involved.

Immoral. Let's get it on the table. People are behaving badly.

People are behaving the way they should not be behaving. Why then do we tend in this seminar to simply say, "Well, that's the way it is. Now let's go on and think of public policies that can compensate for the fact that people are behaving badly." I think the public policies we've got are at least partly to blame for how easy it is to behave badly. The welfare debate is well known. The divorce law debate is well known, just to name perhaps the two most conspicuous examples of situations where the public policies that we've got have reduced the cost and the consequences for behaving immorally.

Public policies that we've got contribute to the problem of fatherlessness. If we want to start dealing with fatherlessness, this "phenomenon" that we have been talking about, we might start by undoing the destructive public policies that we've got that make it easier for immorality and fatherlessness to follow.

Bonnie Thornton Dill, professor of women's studies at the University of Maryland, brings us back again to the question of defining family:

We've blamed mothers, we've blamed fathers, but the issue that we still have not addressed is what we would do as a society if we really wanted to support children and not just the children who look like us but all of the children who are born in the society. A lot of times embedded in the discussion, although not always explicit, is a sense of concern because children who look like us are in danger. Those children who do not look like us, whose mothers do not necessarily conform to the values of the majority, we care less about.

I'm in favor of marriage. I'm married. I have three children. My mother lives with me. I'm doing all kinds of family things, and I believe very much in that. But by the same token we must ask: What definition of family are we working with, and how are we going to support the varieties of families that do exist? Whether we like it or not, we do not live in a society where one set of moral values rules. We are not a homogeneous society in which everybody shares a common set of values. What is moral is to have people who are contributing in a constructive way to the overall well-being of the society.

In a period of tremendous social change and tremendous social disorganization and reorientation, people need help to be able to support their children in constructive ways. Fathers need help to remain engaged in ways that are both financial and emotional. Mothers need the help of the fathers and of community people and support people to raise the children. These are the issues we should be focusing on.

We have started a discussion that is not easily resolved and the points of view are many. We're going to continue. There are values involved, and there has to be a vision of what could be. I am an optimist because I feel as we move toward greater equality, with women and men sharing the burden and sharing the parenting, that there will be less imbalance, less of the hatreds and resentments that are bred from absolute dependence. There will be less taking it out in sexual warfare or on the children.

There might be a renaissance of mutual commitment and responsibility between the sexes, but there will also be a growing acceptance by our whole society of enormous diversity and patterns of family life. There are many ways of loving, and there are many ways of parenting that are good ways. We can't impose just one way. I have been interested in studies of the African American community that show the strength of family structures that do not fit the pattern of mama, papa, and two children. There are structures, for instance, that take care of age in ways that the small nuclear middle-class American family does not. Our thinking has to be open. We can have family values without perhaps thinking only of one kind of family.

THE COMMUNITY CONNECTION

As the new paradigm seminar proceeds, the Committee of 100 collects money for a full-page ad urging the president to veto any welfare bill that eliminates Aid to Families With Dependent Children and food for babies. "An Attack on Poor Women is an Attack on All Women," the ad says. We tell Betsy Myers, who has been put in charge of a new office for women in the White House, that the president has to meet with women leaders before he makes the deal he is rumored to be considering on welfare. He listens to the women in a different way now. Their overwhelming support for his defense of the critical social programs is changing the political map.

An office to monitor violence against women is set up in the Justice Department. But such an office is only a band-aid. We have to get out of this economic bind where only the very rich—and the technological geniuses—get richer, and the rest of us, men and women, in our frustration, turn against each other, manipulated too easily by our own precarious perch on that slippery steep economic slope if we speak up for, identify with, those poorer and those more vulnerable than we.

Too often the so-called debate on family values is a debate about abortion or sexual immorality or divorce, but when we talk about the value of families, we are talking about conditions that support and nurture family values. As Hillary Clinton would say, it takes a community for families to really flourish and to be able to responsibly nurture children in this advanced industrial society that we're living in now. The new paradigm seminar hears some concrete examples of programs that are working.

Harriett Woods, former head of the National Women's Political Caucus and lieutenant governor of Missouri, talks about her work with the Grace Hills Settlement House in St. Louis. The settlement house concept is based on the self-help tradition, which contrasts with the social service concept of more recent times where agencies do things for people by providing services and bringing resources:

At Grace Hills we're using the MORE system, Member Organized Resource Exchange, which is a linkage and referral network that is built around neighborhood councils to bring people together to talk about what is really important to them, what they want to change. It rewards participants with stipends for coming in and becoming trained, perhaps in helping one another, to take care of the older

*people in the neighborhood, to set up self-help in taking care of chil-
dren, creating these extended family kinds of support. They, in turn,
become leaders and gain skills and confidence, and many of them
then go on to be employed in the mainstream of society.*

*Confidence comes with knowing what is going on elsewhere in
the community. There's an amazing percentage of people who now
have computers, or at least have access to them. I was talking to one
woman who began as a single-parent welfare mother, came in for
one of the early training programs, began to become knowledgeable,
and now is the supervisor for neighborhood coordinators, who in
turn are training other women, and she's so proud of the fact. She
said, "Do you have email? I have email. Let me give you my number
and we'll communicate." There was such a sense of power in her feeling that she had command of the same kinds of things that were
valued in the larger society.*

*When we talk about community, we have to make sure that those
people who are supposed to benefit feel that they are contributing as
well.*

*In a time when family stability, particularly for families in dis-
advantaged neighborhoods, is threatened in a very real way, in an
everyday way, in health and environment, violence and lack of advantage and opportunity, we have to be sure that we're talking, yes,
economic opportunities but also the sense of empowerment that
comes when we encourage and reward individuals to be givers as
well as takers—to gain some skills so that they can master the decisions in their own lives and obviously bring about change. When
you can bring about change in the community around you, that af-
fects your own life that makes a difference in how you view your own
future.*

Gary Walker, president of Public/Private Ventures (P/PV), told of
his organization's evaluation of an old institution, Big Brothers and
Big Sisters, and what it implies about community support for family
values. Big Brothers, Big Sisters is ninety-five years old, has never
been evaluated and has always been on the outskirts of public social
policy. P/PV studied a thousand kids in eight cities—500 had Big

Brothers or Sisters, and 500 did not—and did an eighteen-month follow-up:

What each Big Brothers and Big Sisters did in these eight cities was meet with a child three and a half hours a week, three weeks a month, over a period of twelve months. The children were all from single parent families; the parents requested the mentors. In public policy terms it's a modest intervention; in human terms it's considerable: what the adult was giving was three weeks of his or her time over the course of a year on a one-on-one relationship with an unknown child.

We found out that for ten- to fifteen-year-olds—a prime time for young people to start using drugs—there was on average a 40 percent reduction in first-time drug use among those who had mentors. For black males, the reduction was 72 percent, meaning that for every 100 black male teenagers who start using drugs, the addition of a mentor to their lives would reduce the number to 28.

Alcohol reduction was the same; with a mentor it was 30 percent less. With a mentor, school absenteeism declined 50 percent. There was even a small rise in grades, which surprised us because you don't expect improvement in academic performance from a nonacademic intervention. There was a much more optimistic view on the part of the kids who had mentors that they could do well in school in the future. And one of the most interesting findings was that the parent-child relationship improved with the addition of a mentor to the child's life.

Perhaps the most significant implication of this study for public policy is that these mentors were just told to be friends with the youth. They didn't tutor; they weren't drug counselors; they had no "life transforming" objective. They spent time; they developed a trusting relationship; they spent more time. It was adult time and caring, not professionalized services, that got these results.

But good mentoring is not an easy solution. Big Brothers and Big Sisters agencies have ninety years of experience and select mentors very, very carefully. Only thirty-four out of every hundred adults who showed an interest became mentors. They were interviewed *carefully. The program was most concerned about finding adults who would consistently live up to a commitment like that over a year. In screening, working with the kids and the mentor over the next year, and giving both training and oversight, it cost Big Brothers, Big Sisters about $1,000 per relationship per year. This is not a cost-free solution.*

And that leads me to the public financing implications. Between 5 and 15 million kids in this country could use this kind of help right now. If you take the lower number and assume you could cut the cost in half, to $500 a year, and still get the same wonderful impacts, you still need approximately $2.5 billion. There is only one way to get that, and that is if the public sector sees itself as an integral part of the functioning of communities and families. At present we do not have that attitude with any consistency in this country. So in mentoring we have an effective solution to many problems that bother American citizens a lot—and we are not capitalizing on it.

Finally, Kent Amos, formerly a vice president at Xerox Corporation, tells us about his personal experience adopting teenage kids and how this led to his nonprofit Urban Family Institute:

Fifteen years ago I came face to face with the subject matter of today's discussion from a parenting standpoint. When I moved back to Washington, D.C., which is my native home, we decided to put our two children in public schools. What that did was to place our children in the public school paradigm in the middle of an urban center, and we had to do something about the children who surrounded them. To make a long story short, my wife and I adopted eighty-seven teenagers over an eleven year period of time. We took these kids into our home. When you literally have a houseful of kids for more than a decade, it does change your world, I assure you. What it did was to bring the skill set of a corporate executive, one who had been in the military as an officer in Vietnam, to the issue of restructuring the way our society cares for children.

By changing the structures around these teenagers, and by placing demands on them, we were able to help seventy-three of them to go to college. But you don't leave Xerox and the cushy life of a vice president because your children become successful or because people give you awards for what you are doing. It's because you get up one morning and the phone rings and they call you to the hospital. Your sixteen-year-old boy whom you brought into your home in April is now shot down with four bullet holes in him the following February. Then the next year, your nineteen-year-old son, whom you sent off to Northeastern University, comes home from school, plays basketball where you played as a child, and you get called to the playground. There's a boy lying there with a butcher knife in his back, and he bleeds to death.

When you lose a child every year for seven years, you say there is something wrong with a society structurally that produces the kind of chaos that is causing disproportionate numbers of young children to die violently. I was obligated then first as an adult, and secondly as a professional, to deal with the structural question. What my wife and I had been doing by taking children into our home was only an anecdotal solution. It did not address the structural problems which placed our children in danger in the first place. So, the Urban Family Institute was born.

The Institute's purpose is to look structurally at how communities, how society will prepare adults. Secretary of Housing and Urban Development, Henry Cisneros, asked us about eighteen months ago what we would do if we had the responsibility for the Chicago Housing Authority. Of course, the conventional wisdom is that the problem can be solved by blowing up all the buildings and turning them from high-rise to low-rise. The Urban Family Institute holds that it is not a high-rise question. If it were simply a high-rise question, I would agree that you should blow up every building at Cabrini Green. But only if you also go over to Lake Shore Drive and blow up those buildings. Because Lake Shore Drive also has high concentrations of people. In fact, they're building more high-rises along Lake Shore Drive if you know anything about Chicago. So, it is not a question of high-rise, it's a question of what's in the high-rise.

If you believe that there is a capacity within the community to be different, then the question becomes: how do you create the struc-

ture to encourage and promote that difference? How do you make that difference a reality? We said to the secretary, "We have to build structures based on the models that are already in place." Secretary Cisneros asked, "Where is it being done now?" I said, "The University of Chicago does it. The University of Michigan does it every day. Both universities have a system that starts at freshman year and ends up at undergraduate and graduate levels. Large numbers of people process through those university systems. We can design a similar curriculum of transformation for the entire community—a curriculum which could be used to transform Cabrini Green."

The Urban Family Institute is now working with three universities here in the District of Columbia: Howard, U.D.C., and Catholic. We're designing a curriculum of transformation for families living in a public housing site and in the community surrounding it. We're looking at a 10x20 block area that has a university at the bottom of it (Howard), a high school at the top end (Roosevelt), a junior high school (McFarland), three elementary schools, boys and girls clubs, several churches, and public housing projects. All of these will be linked together in a $1.5 million computer network. We're looking at chartering the schools in that community to change the nature of the schools, so that the schools will begin to fit a twenty-first century educational paradigm. School will probably start at 6:00 am and will go to 11:00 pm. All of this will be associated with the community's human development strategy.

We're going to redesign physically the public housing property to accommodate child care, a health and wellness center, adult and child education, access to twenty-first century technology, and recreation activities. For example, we are going to put in a movie theater and a bowling alley. People say, "Why do you want to do that?" Well, the reality of it is there are no bowling alleys in African American communities anywhere in the country let alone Washington, D.C. There are only five motion picture theaters in the entire United States in African American communities. The point to all of this is that you can design intellectually, then install operationally, new paradigms if you can muster the will and the economic resources. It is more a will issue than economics because the cost of it *can be accommodated. We are assessing the costs associated with transferring dollars from the existing delivery systems. Most of these communities are already heavily subsidized in a lot of ways, and we believe that you can shift these subsidies to provide the infrastructure at no additional cost. The real economic benefits are long term, as families move to self-sufficiency. These long term benefits of helping families to help themselves and their children will substantially outweigh the costs of implementation.*

A STAND FOR CHILDREN

There's something very important here. This whole discussion is reaching from different directions to a sense that there has to be a value in this society, in this country, in its public policies, and even in the bottom line private sector, for the lives of people, women, men, and children and for a community. The bowling alleys shouldn't be shut down. The value of community has to take precedence over the short-term, next quarter stock market share. In the 1996–1997 seminar we might deal with new visions of community and corporate power.

How are we going to translate some of the things that we've said into a new paradigm for measuring the bottom line, into a new paradigm for the federal budget or national budget? How are we going to attack this growing disparity in income? More than sixty years ago you had Roosevelt, you had the New Deal. You had a whole era of social policy and social progress. Then it looked like we were going to destroy that with the Contract with America. That hasn't happened. The people don't want that all destroyed, but nobody has come up with a new structure, with the kinds of policies that would lead to the common good as a priority for evolution of democracy. We're not denying the need for business to do well and prosper. We're not denying the importance of individual enterprise or even an enlightened capitalism, which I think is possible. But what kind of public policies are necessary for that?

The backlash is getting serious now. At the Mitsubishi plant near

Peoria, where I grew up, women are filing the gravest, largest suit of sexual harassment ever with the Equal Employment Opportunity Commission, tearing the town apart. Women who have moved into "nontraditional jobs" at this auto plant are being pawed, mauled, called "slut" and "whore" by the men, and not given training they need to do their jobs. These are the only "good" jobs in town. The fury, insecurity of the men is being vented on the women. It's not enough to win the lawsuit, for the women and men in Normal, Illinois.

In the new polls, women around the country are showing increasing concern over what's happening to children, poor people, older people, and families. The Council of Presidents of National Women's Organizations holds a press conference on Capitol Hill warning Congress and the president that the elimination of standards of social welfare by turning Aid to Families with Dependent Children into block grants for the states would be seen by women generally as a betrayal. And this time the major women's organizations are represented as well as women beyond the narrow circle of politically correct feminism—writer Anne Roiphe, who wrote *Up the Sandbox* in 1970, and her daughter Katie Roiphe, whose *The Morning After* book questioning recent feminist focus on date rape and victimhood was attacked by politically correct feminists. But they raise their voices loud and clear for the welfare safety net. Some women still need to emerge from victimhood. But we are talking to ourselves. The media are not covering opposing the attacks on welfare.

And so I suggest that we stop dealing with the issue in isolation. We go to John Sweeney, the new, militant president of the AFL-CIO, and ask labor and the senior citizens organizations angry about Medicaid, and the student groups concerned with education loans, those fighting for children and the churches who are also concerned about the welfare cuts, to join in a common speakout on income inequality, and what it is doing to American families. We begin to move toward a march of not just women, but people of all ages and colors, men and children. I start working with the Grey Panthers and the National Student Association on a summit conference of youth and age, to transcend the danger of intergenerational warfare and merge our own strengths for some common, new priorities. As we go from meeting to meeting, Heidi Hartmann and I and several other women leaders play with slogans "Beyond Greed—The Common Good." "How Many Yachts Can You Buy?"

Sweeney promises to speak at our "income inequality" speakout. He sees the importance of women to the labor movement. In his own union, the Service Employees' International Union (SEIU), most of the new workers, temp workers, and service workers are women. He set up a new AFL-CIO office for women. Karen Nussbaum, founder of "9 to 5," leaves the Clinton administration for the AFL-CIO because she sees this as the next frontier for women: organizing in and with unions. Sweeney tells us maybe union pension funds, maybe women should buy and use stocks to question the downsizing, "raise hell in the shareholders' meetings." Heidi and others are being asked for advice by the Progressive Caucus in the House. Democrats in the Senate and House, and some Republicans turning their backs on Speaker Gingrich, are fighting now to increase the minimum wage.

In various ways, we start to make the new paradigm happen. At Mount Vernon College, where I am now Distinguished Visiting Professor, I lead a symposium series in the spring of 1996 on "Transcending the War Between the Sexes, A New Paradigm for Women and Men." We aim to get beyond the scars and frustrations of old sex roles, sexual politics, and backlash. We deal with the concrete realities of restructuring jobs and family roles in the face of downsizing. We try to articulate new visions of intimacy, power, and success. The American Association of University Women, a member organization of the Council of Presidents of National Women's Organizations, is working with Girl Scouts and Boy Scouts, Girls Clubs and Boys Clubs, to draw up a new social contract for girls and boys to learn and grow together. In Washington, D.C., on Take Your Daughter to Work Day, lots of fathers take their sons.

Then, Marian Wright Edelman makes a conference call to the heads of the major women's organizations, asking them to join her in a call to "Stand for Children" and she is also thinking in terms of that "Million Man March." She does a valiant job of mobilizing the church groups and nonpolitical volunteer and community organizations there is so much talk about lately: "civil society." The AFL-CIO supports the "Stand for Children" as do the women's organizations. We go see her to talk about really mobilizing our forces to make a political statement that can't be ignored, apprehensive as we are about the continued demand from the Republicans, and acquiescence from Clinton now, "to end welfare as we know it." But she is adamant that the "Stand for Children" can't be political.

I get my own grandchildren to join me in the "Stand for Children" that first Saturday in June 1996 hoping that it will be a memorable march, remembering how I brought their parents as children to Washington for Martin Luther King's march and to protest the war in Vietnam. My daughter Emily carried her first child as a baby in her backpack in our last massive woman's march to protest the gag rule on abortion when counselors were told they could not even discuss abortion. Jesse Jackson's people were protective of her baby as the crowds pressed in. Those marches galvanized political dissent and public and political energy.

In the 1990's, in America, the voice of real political dissent seems stilled. No candidate of either party confronts the excesses of corporate greed, the intensifying income inequality and job downsizing that is creating the climate of frustration and rage and fear that fuels a politics of hate. I fear a backlash against the movement for racial and women's equality. "Family values" has become the reactionary fundamentalist battle cry in terms of the new economic realities eroding family security and hopes for our children's future. It would seem to me that we could and must transcend that politics of identity, of separate special interests, and the culture of greed, to protect and keep open the future of all our children.

But the 200,000 who come from "civil society" to "Stand for Children" on that nonpolitical Saturday are ignored. Following directions not to be political, they do not voice the demand that needs to be heard now to save Aid to Families with Dependent Children, foodstamps, and other services needed to keep over a million American children out of poverty. The heads of women's organizations ask me to join them in vigils at the White House, and last minute meetings at the Capitol to protest the threats to children's welfare. But the voice of massive political outrage, led by women, that was heard in the nation when Gingrich shut down the government last year in order to cut Medicare, Medicaid, Head Start, loans for education and protection of the environment—and President Clinton refused to give in—is not heard when Congress ends "welfare as we know it." And the president, to our sorrow, signs that draconian welfare "reform bill," ending Aid to Families with Dependent Children, which according to the government's own statistics will force more than a million children into poverty.

By 1996, the empowerment of women, in the United States and the world, has made a quantum leap. At the Beijing World Conference of Women, not even the fearful authoritarian rulers of China could still 40,000 women of all colors from those voluntary nongovernmental organizations of civil society and movements for equality all over the world who joined the official delegates. These women and men had been fighting for women's equality in their own lands. These were not the second-string male politicians and their wives and secretaries who had populated those UN conferences in the past. They cemented in an official UN document world consensus on a woman's right to control her own sexuality and reproduction, on women's rights as human rights, and on genital mutilation of girls and violence against women in the home or on the street as a violation of human rights. And it was the political empowerment of women the world over that achieved this official worldwide sanction.

In 1996, by a gender gap of 17 percent, women elected the president of the United States, not men and women, now women and men. New statistics revealed that in the U.S. women now receive more than half the bachelor's and master's degrees, make up almost half the labor force, earn almost half the income in a growing number of families, and more Americans now work in companies owned or run by women, than in the Fortune 500. For the first time, a woman is named secretary of state in the United States of America.

In their twenties, entering the labor market, American women now earn almost as much as men. As they start to have children, this changes. By their forties, inequality reasserts itself. But this is a combination of the "glass ceiling"—remaining discrimination against women at the top—and the lack of structures in the job economy that take child-caring into account. And men in their forties now are being hit by downsizing, those college-educated white men whose 20 percent drop in income in this decade alerted me to the need for a new paradigm. For a basic restructuring of our economy is needed now—countering the income inequality, confronting the needs of family that can't be ignored in a workplace where women now equal or outnumber men, and more and more men share the parenting responsibilities. And this restructuring can't be accomplished in terms of women versus men, blacks versus white, old versus young, conservative versus liberal. We need a new political movement in America that puts the lives and interests of people first. It can't be done by separate, single issue movements now, and it has to be political, to protect and translate our new empowerment with a new vision of community, with a new structures of community that open the doors again to real equality of opportunity for the diverse interests of all our children—a new evolution of democracy as we approach the new millennium.

Index

University of Southern California, 7

Sweeney, John, 81, 112, 113

Thomas, Clarence, 11
Toffler, Alvin, 84, 92–3
Toffler, Heidi, 84, 92–3

UAW (United Auto Workers), 29–31
United Nations Fourth World Conference on Women, 81, 115
University of Maryland, 103
University of Southern California, 7, 10
University of Sydney, Australia, 23
Urban Family Institute, 108–11
Urban Institute, 14, 35, 55, 56, 60, 86, 91, 93
U.S. Department of Labor Women's Bureau, 91
U.S. News & World Report, 84

Voice of America, 40

Walker, Gary, 106–8
Warren, James, 65, 67

Warren Bennis Leadership Institute, University of Southern California, 10
Washington Post, 48, 84, 93
Washington Times, 66, 84
Weitzman, Lenore, 101
Wellesley College, 45
Wider Opportunities for Women, 14, 23, 56
Wilkins, Roger, 89
Wilson, William Julius, 90
Women, Men, and Media Project, 65–6
Women in Poverty Project, 23
Women's Legal Defense Fund, 33
Woodhull, Nancy, 65
Woodrow Wilson International Center for Scholars, 11, 15
Woods, Harriett, 57, 105–6
Work and Family Institute, 44

Xerox, 62, 108
Xerox Canada, 75

Yettaw, David, 29–31, 32
YWCA, 140